SWIMMING
IN YOUR BRAIN

AuthorHouse™
1663 Liberty Drive
Bloomington, IN 47403
www.authorhouse.com
Telephone: 1-800-839-8640

Published by AuthorHouse   8/24/2015

First Editor: Naomi Long, *The Artful Editor*
Second Editor: Elle A. Simon

Library of Congress Control Number: 2014913547
Simon, Elle A.
Swimming in Your Brain
A Practicum to the Inner Guide Meditation,
A Spiritual Technology for the 21st Century

ISBN 978-1-4969-1529-0 (sc) and
ISBN 978-1-4969-1528-3 (e)

Print information available on the last page.

Typeset in: Papyrus
Printed on acid-free paper.

Permissions granted from Redwheel/Weiser to use certain information and images from *The Inner Guide Meditation* by Edwin Steinbrecher.

Permissions also granted from all individuals depicted in the astrological charts used and remarks about those charts.

Astrological Symbols by Halloran Software
Astrological Charts by Matrix Software

Dedication

To the memory of Edwin Steinbrecher
(April 4, 1930–January 26, 2002)
Uranian Power and Fixed Adept
He showed me the path to being all of myself
through this amazing compass.

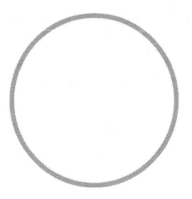

Circle of Hands
Balancing the Spirit of all Inner Guides with all Earthly inhabitants

With deep gratitude and love to
My Inner Guide and Archetypes, my anchors;
My Parents for bringing me to paradise – Earth
(Father: Uranian Power and Earth Adept; Mother: Plutonian Vessel and Uranian Instrument);
My Talented Immediate and Extended Family
Flora and Leonard
Brandy
Chunlin
Xin Sheng

In grateful acknowledgment to
Those who worked with Ed
to bring his IGM creation into practical reality for all of us

With great appreciation to
Those who have permitted me to use their natal charts in this Workbook
My amazing Friends/Clients/Students, past/present
all of whom inspire _me_ to be closer to Center

Also to
Kepler College of Astrological Arts & Sciences
Rob
Maureen
To the USC, CAAS Department
My Moonlinks Teachers
in many books, classes, seminars, workshops, and in life; and
Family Friends, who bring warmth and just plain fun, the _juice_ to do my work.

SWIMMING
IN YOUR BRAIN

A Practicum to The Inner Guide Meditation
A Spiritual Technology for the 21st Century

Elle A. Simon

authorHOUSE®

Reading Guide

Preface

Swimming in Your Brain provides an organized system in three stages of development for the journey to your Center through the Inner Guide Mediation, as presented by Edwin C. Steinbrecher in his book, *The Inner Guide Meditation –A Spiritual Technology for the 21st Century* (Revised Sixth Edition, Samuel Weiser, Inc., York Beach, Maine, 1989).

Even though it is preferable to be initiated into the Inner Guide Meditation by someone who studied with Ed Steinbrecher before his passing, or with someone at D.O.M.E., the meditation center, before it closed in December 2002, we can take nothing away from the value of being introduced to his innovative meditation technique for helping us stay on purpose toward manifesting what is *true* for us, as individuals, through the basics of meeting our Guide starting on page 53 of Ed's book.

This book, *Swimming in Your Brain*, provides templates for life-long meditation using the technique introduced by Ed, with the understanding that one's personal IGM is an evolving process. Starting from age 7, generally everyone can begin to consciously integrate their Archetypes into daily life.

Even before you're initiated into the IGM, you may wish to start this work by meeting and building a relationship with your Shadows (see page 16); then, after either being initiated into the IGM or doing a self-initiation (see the suggested Initiation Outline Template on page 38), you may want to add connecting with your Archetypes for each Sign of the daily Moon (see page 45), as well as with the Archetypes who are your Consciousness Resistant Factors, if you have any (see pages 22-23).

From there, as your confidence builds and you get better acquainted with your Archetypes, you'll no doubt begin to work on specific "problems" (see *When you Work on Problems* page 113.) Eventually, you will find it extremely valuable to understand and know how to work with your Archetypes as they move through your birth chart by Astrological Transits (see Chapter 12, page 89), and learning the uses of the *I Ching* with your Basic Archetypes/Board of Directors (pages 134-136).

As well as a practical guide to the use of the Inner Guide Meditation, this book brings additional Energy Influences for navigating this life experience, all of which are compatible with and supported by the Inner Guide Meditation. You are invited to use this book to learn more about working on the Inner Plane to bring greater fulfillment on the Outer Plane. There's no *intermediary* – <u>you and your Archetypes</u> work together to determine your course of action from a personal, spiritually superior approach.

Are you ready to have your brain rewired?
(*Take your time* – and, also, <u>schedule</u> it!)

Time is wealth!

Don't squander it.
I'm just sayin'.

Introduction

This book is <u>all</u> about getting closer and closer to Center –
advancing in life and in spiritual consciousness.

My own involvement with the *Inner Guide Meditation* (IGM) began in 1992 when I went to see Ed for what I intended to be professional information gathering and to get his take on my chart. An Astrologer myself, I heard through the grapevine Ed was a good Astrologer – I had not heard anything else.

To my amazement, Ed began asking me about my family members, as "barometers" for what was going on in <u>my</u> life. As I gave him names, he entered them on my birth chart. I thought to myself, and then said, "This isn't what I came here for." After a few brief comments that interested me beyond a chart reading, he told me to close my eyes and enter a cave without "watching" myself. He asked a lot of questions about the cave and then took me on an inner journey I didn't want to end. I was hooked!

Those who've already been initiated into the IGM, will appreciate that <u>my</u> shadow was Casper, the ghost. I couldn't even get to the "two" shadows we have (and some people have *four*!). Obviously, I had a long way to go to have *healthy* Shadows, let alone fully conscious and equal silent partners. Female shadows represent the female side of the ego, and male shadows represent the male side of the ego, and having neither says a lot about my ego at that time.

Since that time, regular meditation has proven its worth in my overall well-being and decision-making ability. My *Inner* work continues to inform how I operate in my *Outer* world. The IGM brings additional *"tools"* through my Archetypes to enhance other opportunities for personal growth. I trained with Ed and other D.O.M.E. instructors to be an Initiator/Counselor of the Inner Guide Meditation, and I encourage people to begin a sustainable process of inner growth and outer progress with the IGM. We have all the answers inside ourselves – we just need a tool to get them out and working for us. <u>This one works</u>! *Swimming in Your Brain* offers an organized system for life-time use of the IGM, as well as other tools for *Inner* and *Outer* progress.

All other books referenced throughout are listed in the Appendix "Additional Reading Opportunities."

Let's go swimming . . .

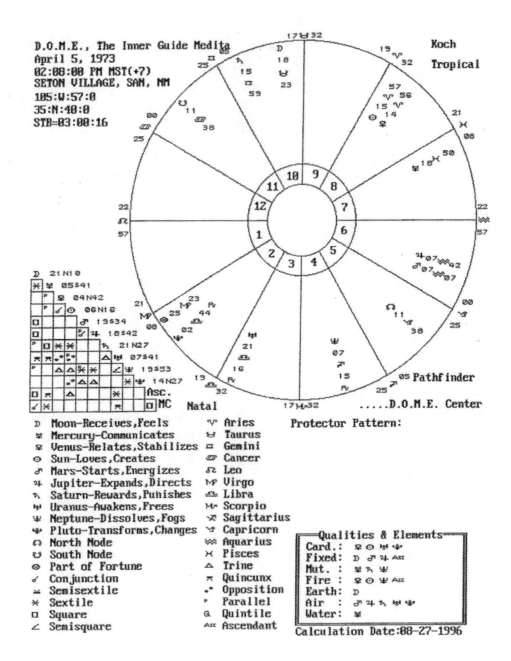

D.O.M.E., The Inner Guide Medita
April 5, 1973
02:06:00 PM MST(+7)
SETON VILLAGE, SAN, NM
105:W:57:0
35:N:40:0
STB=03:00:16

Koch

Tropical

Pathfinder

.....D.O.M.E. Center

Natal

Protector Pattern:

☽ 21 N10
☿ 05S41
♀ 04N42
☉ 06N16
♂ 13S34
♃ 18S42
♄ 21 N27
♅ 07S41
♆ 19S53
♇ 14N27
Asc.
MC

☽	Moon—Receives,Feels		♈	Aries
☿	Mercury—Communicates		♉	Taurus
♀	Venus—Relates,Stabilizes		♊	Gemini
☉	Sun—Loves,Creates		♋	Cancer
♂	Mars—Starts,Energizes		♌	Leo
♃	Jupiter—Expands,Directs		♍	Virgo
♄	Saturn—Rewards,Punishes		♎	Libra
♅	Uranus—Awakens,Frees		♏	Scorpio
♆	Neptune—Dissolves,Fogs		♐	Sagittarius
♇	Pluto—Transforms,Changes		♑	Capricorn
☊	North Node		♒	Aquarius
☋	South Node		♓	Pisces
⊕	Part of Fortune		△	Trine
☌	Conjunction		⊼	Quincunx
⊻	Semisextile		⚹	Opposition
✳	Sextile		∥	Parallel
□	Square		Q	Quintile
∠	Semisquare		Asc	Ascendant

Qualities & Elements
Card.: ♀ ☉ ♅ ♆
Fixed: ☽ ♂ ♃ Asc
Mut. : ☿ ♄ ♆
Fire : ♀ ☉ ♆ Asc
Earth: ☽
Air : ♂ ♃ ♄ ♅ ♆
Water: ☿

Calculation Date:08-27-1996

CHAPTER ONE

JUST WHAT IS THE "INNER GUIDE MEDITATION"?

"Meditations are *actions* that produce results on the planet."
Ed

First and foremost, the Inner Guide Meditation is a gift from Ed Steinbrecher to us. Those who diligently use it have a lifetime of blessings working with their Archetypes on the Inner Plane to navigate life on the Outer Plane beyond linear thinking. Discovered in August 1968, the meditation raises one's consciousness toward greater personal contribution for the good of all.

This is a practical spiritual technique for getting valuable information from our unconscious mind and involves active imagination, Archetypes, Astrology, Tarot, Kabbalah, and I Ching. It is not about "quieting the mind." These time-tested tools have been combined by Ed to give us a meditation for working on our Inner Plane. This technique opens choices in our life experience and enables us to have more control of our life.

The Inner Guide Meditation is based on people in our reality as they are found in specific areas of our personal birth chart. Our point of view repeats according to our relationships with these people, and issues we may have with them can be healed in this meditation.

Our main Inner Guide comes to teach us a way to access spirit and creative forces within us. Through the meditation, we experience and communicate with our Inner Guides, who give us the love, protection, and guidance no one on the Outer Plane could hope to give over our lifetime. They subtly direct us toward our own Inner spiritual goals. They neither tell us what someone else is thinking or doing, nor do they tell us to do anything that would harm ourselves or someone else. The meditation enhances our value system and balances materiality with spirituality.

The archetypes in our Inner world are neutral living aspects of Spirit within us; each appearing in a way our individual egos can experience and understand what they are willing to communicate to us if we ask. They can influence our behavior, in general, and our responses to projections. They may not tell us what we want to hear, but they will never tell us to do anything that will harm us, and they will never tell us anything that will help or harm someone else.

Let's go swimming . . .

You might find it useful to peruse the following specific pages in Ed's book.
These page numbers are based on the Revised Sixth Edition of
The Inner Guide Mediation, A Spiritual Technology for the 21st Century

Q & A
Reference

D.O.M.E.
(Dei Omnes Munda Edunt)
All the Gods/Goddesses Bring Forth the Worlds
And
The Inner Guide Meditation

The Initiators' Creed

This I know: the flow of universal energies through me and my response to this flow creates my personal reality. Bringing myself and these energies into harmony heals my experienced world. The inner worlds generate the outer world, and the source of all is within. The Inner Guides are our teachers and advisors in our personal quests for wholeness and spiritual enlightenment. Work with these inner teachers in the Inner Guide Meditation facilitates achievement of these goals. Each of us carries total responsibility, without blame, for the world that is individually experienced and cannot disclaim responsibility for any portion of it. Work with the Inner Guides can bring this world into a state of harmony and balance. To kill, injure or cause harm, either physical or psychological, to a fellow being injures and causes harm to the individual God-flow. Expansion of individual consciousness expands the consciousness of all beings.

Ed Steinbrecher

CHAPTER TWO

ASTROLOGY

Heads Up!
We still have free will!
<u>Awareness</u> is all!

Astrology is a symbolic language designed to accurately describe the internal archetypal energy coding that creates, regulates, and sustains your experienced reality within and without. It is an evolving system that must adjust to human evolution and each individual's level of consciousness. Some of the methods of interpretation have been with us for thousands of years and originate in our pre-historical past.

It is a tool for looking more closely at our opportunities and obstacles and a door opener to living life fully. It's like the gravity that acts as a magnet. We have a say in what the archetypes in our own makeup are telling us. It is a metaphysical science that is a confirmation of who we are and roadmap to our destiny.

Ed Steinbrecher
D.O.M.E.
Initiator's Workbook
August 29, 1996

The Zodiac

The "belt" centered on the ecliptic and divided into 12 arcs of 30° each, where the Signs are shown.
(*The Arkana Dictionary of Astrology* by Fred Gettings, 1985)

Symbols and Sign Names

	Symbols and Sign Names	Elements
♈	Aries	Fire
♉	Taurus	Earth
♊	Gemini	Air
♋	Cancer	Water
♌	Leo	Fire
♍	Virgo	Earth
♎	Libra	Air
♏	Scorpio	Water
♐	Sagittarius	Fire
♑	Capricorn	Earth
♒	Aquarius	Air
♓	Pisces	Water

Luminaries

		Ruler Of	
☉	Sun	♌ Leo	
☽	Moon	♋ Cancer	

Planets

		Ruler Of	
☿	Mercury	♊ Gemini	♍ Virgo
♀	Venus	♉ Taurus	♎ Libra
♂	Mars	♈ Aries	♏ Scorpio
♃	Jupiter	♐ Sagittarius	♓ Pisces
♄	Saturn	♑ Capricorn	♒ Aquarius
♅	Uranus	♒ Aquarius	
♆	Neptune	♓ Pisces	
♇	Pluto	♏ Scorpio	

Some Keywords for Zodiac Signs and Horoscope Houses
The Inner Guide Meditation takes us to that higher place
in our Inner Plane for expression on the Outer Plane.

The *Sign* descriptions below correspond with a "Flat" chart (not necessarily your birth chart). <u>Your</u> chart will likely have other *Signs* on the House cusps (dividing line between each House), as it is the date, time, and coordinates of one's birth that make up the individual chart map and then open the door for deeper exploration. Given that all 12 *Signs* are in all birth charts, we may share some of these traits; however, the *Sign* descriptions given here can be taken into consideration only with someone's entire birth chart data by a professional Astrologer.

As you begin working with transits and aspects, you will see nuances between opportunities and challenges – with nothing being just black or white. References to the Moon below are to the daily Moon-Sign transits. As you begin paying attention to the Energy Influences each day, starting with daily Moon transits, you'll notice the consistency of shifting energies and how we are affected every month when the Moon transits the same *Signs*. This awareness will be useful for planning and scheduling.

For purposes of this meditation, it is beneficial to meditate with the pertinent Archetypes to operate at the higher vibration. They are exceedingly helpful if we ask for suggestions for perfecting how we operate (which will never be easy but certainly more gratifying if we try), especially when our Consciousness Resistant Factors (CRFs) are *unblocked*.

Aries♈   Fire   This is a competitive, spontaneous, and enthusiastic energy. Someone with an Aries Sun can be a courageous trailblazing leader – an entrepreneur. Aries is also related to, among many other things, adventure, action, and the avant-garde. Operating at a lower vibration, those with an Aries Sun have a harder time following through with plans and promises. Using Moon transits to and from the *Sign* of Aries and/or planets/luminaries in Aries, we will learn when we're most vulnerable to operating from the lower vibration. **During an Aries Moon**, people may be crude and insulting, though it's usually unintentional. People are generally more aggressive and can take reasonable risks and win. Aries is related to cerebral hemispheres of the brain, and there may be head-related health concerns and inflammatory diseases.

First House: This is the House of ego, who we think we are – the personality one wants to show (especially in public); one's outlook on life; and how one starts things. This House concerns general health, the physical body, head and eyes, in particular. It may also show what we fear we are <u>not</u> with respect to Inner resources/talents and/or the kind of effort we are likely to put into finding and using our Inner resources.

Taurus♉	Earth	This energy is about endurance, determination, and a strong desire for a "better" life, with gourmet tastes in food, wine, fine jewelry, clothes, and fragrances. Those with a Taurus Sun also demonstrate a strong financial sense with practical thinking in some areas and extravagance in others, along with good common sense. They are romantic, sensual, tactile, and have acute survival needs. There is often a greater interest and talent in music and the arts in general. Operating at a lower vibration, a Taurus may bully, be uncouth, be gluttonous, drink too much, and be a serious gossiper. **Under a Taurus Moon**, people may bully or take a stand against being bullied; they may also show politeness, live "the good life" to the extent possible, and show discipline along with stubbornness. The neck and throat are sensitive areas.

Second House: Inner talents and income earned from them are shown here. It is also the House of one's personal values, possessions, negotiable assets, stocks, ears, mouth, thyroid gland, throat, and vocal organs. This House is where we figure out what Inner resources we have and how to communicate them in our Outer World.

Gemini♊	Air	Optimism and intelligence are linked to opportunism under Gemini. Common traits include versatility, the ability to adapt to the energy of the group and the moment, and usually some writing ability. In just about every area of the Gemini Sun's life, there is a strong need for variety. Operating at a lower vibration, "truth" and promises may be for the moment only, with cunning cleverness and erratic changes of mind. Health concerns involve arms, shoulders, respiratory system, and nerve function. **When the Moon is in Gemini**, the energy is *lighter*, and people are more congenial than usual – at least in the moment. One tool for specific use during the Gemini Moon is the opportunity to think by comparison with greater clarity before choosing between two of anything. For example: What does it look like if I decide to purchase this particular item for my own purposes? And, what does it look like if I use that money for a contribution to a non-profit organization so its value can be stretched beyond myself? Another one might be to look at the worst that could happen if I decide to take a particular action and, if I take that action, whether I could handle the worst-case scenario.

Third House: This House is most closely associated with one's thought processes, communication, speech, writings/writers of technical and/or fictional material, local travel, vehicle, early education, siblings (especially the first sibling), lungs, hands, arms, and shoulders. Our fears and resentments about siblings, family, and home environment can often be seen here.

Cancer ♋	Water	The Sign of Cancer relates to our nurturing and protective instincts, our receptivity in general, and our sensitivity to others. Those with a Cancer Sun sign are concerned with home, food, and family first. They strive to anticipate outcomes before taking action. Operating at a lower vibration, those with a Cancer Sun may be over-protective and operate from a particular bias. **When the Moon is in Cancer,** our spirits are most easily nurtured with great cuisine and copious amounts of encouragement from friends and family. People will tend to be more cliquish and clinging. Health issues often concern stomach and digestive organs.

Fourth House: This House is all about home, emotional foundation, security needs, family, properties, stomach, lower ribs, and breasts. In the IGM, it is the House connected with Mother. Other sources indicate the association with the parent who carries the least influence, and still other sources relate the 4th House to the Mother of one born with the Sun above the horizon, and the Father of one born with the Sun below the horizon. This Astrologer bases the correlation on discussion with the native about his or her relationship with both parents and aspects to/from the 4th House. Fears to be addressed concern confidence in one's creative self-expression, emotional well-being of one's children, and one's emotional fortitude for taking risks.

Leo ♌	Fire	Children, entertainment, and pleasure, in general, are most associated with the Sign of Leo. Those with a Leo Sun strive to be number one, with a title to match. Where we find Leo in our chart, we also find creativity and romance. Operating at a lower vibration, the Leo is arrogant, disloyal, and prevaricates for seemingly no reason. **Under a Leo Moon,** drama kings and queens come out of the woodwork with off-the- wall flashes of anger they get over in a flash, once acknowledged. On the other side, however, there is usually more fun in the atmosphere (and a good time for a party). Everyone wants to be the center of attention, and there are more pride-based responses in communications. Health concerns often involve stress, the dorsal region of the spine, and the heart.

Fifth House: Whatever planet or luminary is in or transiting the 5th House, the focus is on creativity, children, friends where there are expectations, romance, gambling, sports, and entertainment. Physiologically, the cardiac region, spleen, and upper back are vulnerable. Psychologically, we may fear the health implications and outcomes from the risks we take.

Virgo♍	Earth	The Sign of Virgo is associated with strong critical thinking and logic. Where we find Virgo in one's chart, we are likely to find methodical reasoning, meticulous attention to detail, and concern with meeting perfection. Those with a Virgo Sun sign are often service-oriented, focused on hygiene and cleanliness, and are considerate of those closest to them. Operating at a lower vibration, a Virgo may operate with a double standard and be hypercritical of others. There is a tendency to complicate things unnecessarily. Hypochondria and possessiveness may be issues. **In a Virgo Moon**, people are prone to worrying more than usual, and criticism could alternate with vague and manipulative communications. Health issues concern nutrition and the lower abdominal area.

Sixth House: This House represents service provided to us and service we provide to others, usually in our daily job routine. It is associated with one's job, co-workers, hygiene, small/domestic animal companions, illness/disease, dietary needs, and one's intestines. This is the House where we might fear failure in our daily job and how that could affect our relationships – one-to-one, contractual, and public.

Libra♎	Air	The energies that best describe the Sign of Libra include compromise, fairness, harmony, social refinement, lasting relationships/partnerships, teamwork, give and take, high ideals, creativity, and mediation. Those whose Sun Sign is Libra never seem to lose a youthful appearance. One whose Sun is Libra can more easily hear and assess all points of view. When they appear indecisive or express a deviating point of view, they may be attempting to balance discussions. Operating at the lower vibration of Libra, they are inclined to compromise *themselves*; they may hold the negative perspective of others just to get along with them. Staying true to their idealism or not wanting to offend certain people for personal or political reasons may result in taking negative actions that put others in a compromising situation and/or cause hurt feelings. **When the Moon is in Libra**, people exhibit more refinement, greater social skills, and artistic creativity. There may be kidney concerns.

Seventh House: Our Shadows (silent partners), partners on the Outer Plane, one's spouse, roommates, strangers, and open enemies are all located in the 7th House. It also represents contracts/agreements, kidneys, the bladder, and the small of one's back. Fears of intimacy and/or joint finances can be harbored in this House.

Scorpio ♏︎   Water   When we look at what the Scorpio Sign most exhibits, we see passion/intensity, secrecy, research capabilities, healthy skepticism, psychic feelings, strong business sense, and some who are kind to a fault. Those who operate at a lower vibration of the Scorpio Sun may have to keep integrity in check, and sometimes arbitrariness is just for the sake of being arbitrary. There may also be a lack of common sense, power struggles involving shared material and emotional resources, and jealousy issues. **Under a Scorpio Moon**, people tend to be more intense/passionate and have an all-or-nothing attitude. There may be reproductive, elimination, or regenerative difficulties.

Eighth House: The 8th House indicates one's joint emotional and material resources, regenerative ability, passions, sex energy, powers of transformation, legacy, inheritance, debts, insurance, and taxes. It also concerns the pelvis, gonads, the reproductive system, colon, and rectum. Psychological indications relate to the effects of sharing joint resources or one's personal rituals and/or publishing aspirations.

Sagittarius ♐︎   Fire   The Sagittarius Sign most closely represents "truth-seeking," curiosity, experimentation, companionship, and shared experiences. Conversations with a Sagittarius Sun Sign can cover many subjects, with a particular emphasis on higher education, philosophy, foreign affairs and travel, as well as environmental concerns. Those operating at a lower vibration may play "gotcha" to provoke an argument, and there may be a tendency toward self-righteousness and trying to show superior intellect. They may need to use extra caution to make responsible choices, and temper "brutal honesty" with a spiritually superior approach in sensitive issues. **In a Sagittarius Moon**, people are inclined to reach out to those with whom they want to maintain a connection; there's a greater focus on foreign affairs, higher education, and legal issues. There may be particular issues with thighs, hips, and the sciatic nerve.

Ninth House: In the 9th House the emphasis is on higher education, expansion of consciousness, publishing, the law, Universal laws, legal system, judges, legal matters, teaching above high school level, foreign travel, long journeys, foreign affairs, foreign people, religion, philosophy, spiritual path, and mysticism; and it is the Ascendant of our first Inner Guide, where we see his appearance and personality. Fears often loom large about preparation for one's career achievement and reputation.

Capricorn ♑ Earth The Capricorn *Sign* is associated with strong ambitions, status seeking, using all resources well (including their time), diplomacy, pessimism mixed with dry wit, maturity, and responsibility. Those with a Capricorn Sun strive to be part of the established class. They may be color-blind (seeing beige and gray easiest), and have a tendency toward absent-mindedness, though they generally do have good memories. They are often good athletes. Capricorn males are generally quite amorous, most often interested in classic automobiles, and are particularly dutiful to their Mother's well-being. Those operating at a lower vibration of the Capricorn Sun are often more calculating, controlling, and are social climbers who use others to advance their own social status. **Under a Capricorn Moon**, people may also have dietary issues involving *living to eat and drink* versus *eating to live*; they may be more absent-minded than usual, and must release/shift fear and pessimism to responsible action.

Tenth House: This is the House of social destiny, ambition, career, worldly attainment, fame, authority figures, the government, employer/user, reputation, and rules. It is the House most associated with Father. Other sources indicate it as the House of the parent who carries the most influence, and still other sources relate the 10th House to the Father of one born with the Sun below the horizon and the Mother of one born with the Sun above the horizon. This Astrologer bases the correlation on discussion with the native about his or her relationship with both parents and aspects to/from the 10th House planets or luminaries. The 10th House also relates to the knees, cartilage, bones, teeth, and gall bladder. Fear of one falling from grace in the minds of group members with whom we are associated.

Aquarius ♒ Air Keywords for Aquarius include altruism, arrogance, originality, deep thinking, a scientific bent, iconoclastic, greater political sensibilities, and social change. Those with an Aquarius Sun who tend to operate at a lower vibration cannot be held to personal expectations or specific times for phone calls or get-togethers. **Under an Aquarius Moon** people surprise each other and are often more innovative. They are frequently attracted to abstract art, and avant-garde and/or electric music. Physical ailments include cramps in calves, ankles, heart irregularities, and nerve disorders.

Eleventh House: The 11th House reflects society as the collective. It shows one's attraction to certain types of social affairs, and legislation, the lower legislative branches, idealism, hopes, wishes, and goals (measured by death), memberships, groups to which one is attracted, acquaintances, electrical systems, and airplanes. It relates to blood circulation and psychologically relates to fears about hidden enemies over which we have no control.

Pisces ♓   Water   Among other things, where we find Pisces in our chart, we are likely to find an emphasis on escape, image and/or imagery, artistry, feet, the sea, large charitable institutions, as well as one's long-range vision. Those with a Pisces Sun may have higher spiritual powers, and be more sympathetic, sentimental, and sensitive than other Sun signs. Operating at a lower vibration, there can be a tendency to blame others instead of taking responsibility for misfortune; there can be cruelty, deceit, cheating, and conspiracy. Health concerns are related to addictions, liver, and feet. **When the Moon is in Pisces**, people generally alternate between work-a-holism and the need to escape into fantasy, between meanness and sympathy, insecurity and confidence, self-pity and benevolence, selfishness and selflessness. They tend to be more comfortable in familiar surroundings. It is a time when impressions can get in the way of facts, and things are generally not as they seem in the moment. It's a great time to write poetry, take photographs, go fishing, or go to a movie.

Twelfth House: We *swim* in the subconscious mind, which rules most of what is associated with the 12th House: sleep, karmic responsibilities, seclusion, escapism, secrets, dreams, dreamers, the past, secret societies, hidden enemies, privacy needs, retirement, informers/spies, scandal, self-undoing, self-destruction, drug addiction, misfortune, trials, prisons, hospitals, places of solitude, thieves, theft, schemers, swindlers, treachery, unseen or unexpected troubles. If these matters are not met head-on, confidence tanks.

Quick-Reference Keywords for Planets and Luminaries. . .
Their Energy Influences

Planets are actors that seek to express through the Houses and the *Signs* they rule.
Awareness is all.

This list can be used for a general sense of the Energy Influences of the Archetypes in Houses where there are specific problems. For additional keywords, see *Tarot –Archetype Essences* (pages 45-47) and *Some Keywords for Zodiac Signs and Horoscope Houses* (pages 6-12).

Planets	Sign Ruled	Archetype	Energy Influences
♂ Mars	Aries ♈ Scorpio ♏	Tower	Ego energy, physical action, vitality, fire, explosive; health issues with muscles, fevers, blood
♀ Venus	Taurus ♉ Libra ♎	Empress	Creativity, socialness, attraction (affection, love, money), relaxation; throat, thyroid, and kidneys
☿ Mercury	Gemini ♊ Virgo ♍	Magician	Mental focus, memory, the connector, all communications, short-distance travel, nerves, lungs/respiratory system, small intestine
Luminary ☽ Moon	Cancer ♋	High Priestess	Emotions, what we want to nurture, unconscious attitudes, unconscious behavior; stomach, breasts, diaphragm, uterus
Luminary ☉ Sun	Leo ♌	Sun	Where we want to shine, solar energy (of the physical body); heart, circulatory system

♇ Pluto	Scorpio ♏	Judgment	Transformation, intensity, power struggles; Pluto both creates and destroys, renovation, evolution, deeply hidden elements, sexuality; the colon, reproductive organs
♃ Jupiter	Sagittarius ♐	Wheel of Fortune	Knowledge, beneficence, inclusion, expansion, self-indulgence, law, philosophy, higher-mind education, government; obesity hips, liver, pancreas
♄ Saturn	Capricorn ♑ Aquarius ♒	World	Structure, tests, authority figures, limitations, responsibility, fears, depression, absent-mindedness; bones including teeth, joints
♅ Uranus	Aquarius ♒	Fool	Freedom, great awakener, the unusual, unexpected, sudden, radical change, new; nervous system, spasms, electrical shocks, paralysis, radiation poisoning
♆ Neptune	Pisces ♓	Hanged Man	Reversing your perspective, dreams, unfinished business, leaks, film, poetry, painting, oil, dissolution, deception, delusion, escapism, addictions, illusion, ego-denying, martyr/self-sacrifice, discouragement, confusion, the unreal, the ideal, insecurity; cerebrospinal fluid, lymphatic system, obscure diseases, alcoholism, toxic conditions

CHAPTER THREE

REWIRING YOUR BRAIN

Our Silent Partners...
The earlier in life you meet them
the more they grow with you and help you.
If you've ever had *imaginary* playmates as a child,
your Shadows are your grownup imaginary lifetime silent partners.

Our Shadows represent our <u>unconscious</u> "other half" and are our most important Archetypes – without question! The 7th House of the birth chart reflects our Shadows – who and what we project onto others if we don't give <u>ourselves</u> what we need. We can meet our Shadows (and meet <u>with</u> them) without our Guide's presence and at any time before initiation into the IGM. The objective is to have our Shadows in balance and harmony with our ego (the Ascendant/1st House of our birth chart). Our life on the Outer Plane reflects the balance of our Shadows. <u>Their</u> needs cannot be ignored, and they need to be asked on a daily basis what those needs <u>are</u> in order for them to be our fully <u>conscious</u> and equal silent partners. In response, they do not ask us to do what is impossible or unrealistic.

Your Shadows must be made conscious friends
before your ego can achieve stability with your Center and other aspects of yourself.
To the extent we are specific about what we ask of our Shadows,
the easier our life can be on the Outer Plane.

(Don't be shocked if you see your Inner progress *outside* yourself, first.)

The more you work with your Shadows, the greater your own progress.
Examples of how they can be great partners include the following:

- If there is a confusing situation, ask, "Are you seeing something I am not, right now? Please show me."
- Ask them to stay with you in one-to-one interactions.
- You could ask what they want you to wear on any given day.
- Ask them to keep your ego intact.
- Ask them to keep you from self-sabotage.
- They keep things moving in your life.
- Ask them to help stop you from stealing energy from the possibility your life <u>is</u>.
- Ask them to bring helpful strangers in any given situation. (The more often we meditate with them, they will start serendipitously bringing helpful strangers.)
- They know everything we don't.
- We can have practical meditations with our Shadows regarding money and career plans, to be confirmed with our Basic Archetypes/Board of Directors through I Ching.

Meeting Your Shadows

1. Be seated in an upright position with your eyes closed, your arms and legs unfolded.

2. Visualize any landscape.

3. Invite a male shadow and a female shadow to take their most conscious form within you.

4. Notice what these figures are wearing (if either one or both do not look good, there may be a reason).

5. If your Shadow figure or figures <u>do not</u> look good, ask what is needed to do something new or different, or what it is you need to <u>stop</u> doing, so there is healing and so they are integrated as a conscious part <u>of</u> you and conscious partners <u>for</u> you.

6. Ask the one or both to take a new, healed form.

7. Tell them they would make incredibly good partners for you.

8. Ask what they need from you to be your friends and conscious equal partners.

Balance this new energy by holding hands with your Shadows.
Give them permission to balance their energies within each other and within you.

9. Ask them what names you should call them.

10. They will keep things moving if you connect with them daily.

11. As you work with them, lower back pain and relationship issues are likely to at least begin to heal.

12. Thank them, give them a hug, and let them go, for now.

When your Shadows show they are conscious, and
you experience them as your Equal Silent Partners,
<u>thank</u> them!

MALE NATAL CHART

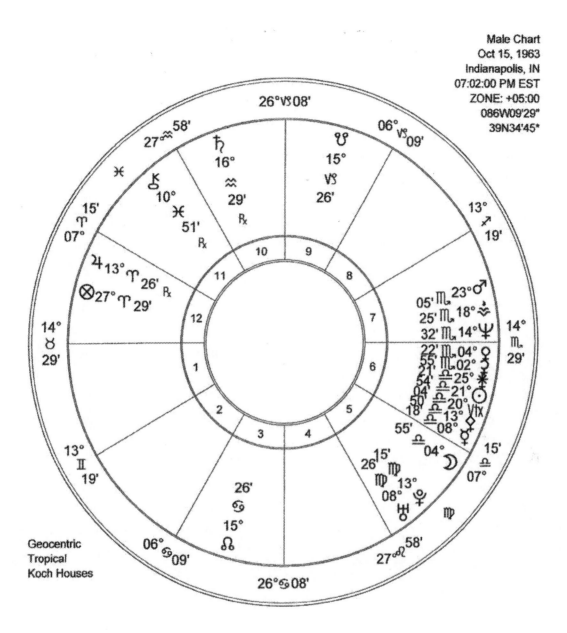

Chart Highlights of a Libra Male Protector
Our Shadows and Projections

The Protector and Alien Energy Construct individuals identified in this book as
Female or Male are based on descriptions in *The Inner Guide Meditation* (pages 217-228).

The chart on the preceding page *glows* with the Libra (♎) male "Protector" (someone without
Alien patterns) who happens to be surrounded by females at home and at work. His Shadows can
be particularly useful because of projection issues from the 7th House (for everyone), which is Ruled
by Libra on a "Flat" chart. But for two quintiles (**Q**) to his 7th House Mars (♂), and one to Neptune
(♆), volatility and serious misunderstandings would likely create havoc in these relationships. The
quintiles (**Q**) to Uranus (♅) and Pluto (♇) in Virgo (♍), conjunct in his 5th House, show him to be
exceptionally capable of handling the constant changes and unusual situations these particular one-
to-one relationships bring, requiring his utmost flexibility and compromise, without compromising
himself.

When Venus (♀), Ruler of his Libra (♎) Sun (☉) and Taurus (♉) Ascendant (Asc) (therefore his
Chart Ruler), is an <u>un</u>blocked Consciousness Resistant Factor (page 22), this Protector presents as
a creative, calm, and charming man. His standout 2nd decan (Taurus/Virgo) on the Ascendant, with a
Libra (♎) dwad, adds to his persona as fair, logical, and persuasive.

The two yods, one action-point being Pluto (♇) in Virgo (♍) and the other Jupiter (♃) in Aries
(♈), show us a Protector with a "mission" to have a child (he and his wife have a daughter) <u>and</u> to use
his many talents in service to the larger whole.

The T-square focal point to his Saturn (♄) in its own 10th House from his Ascendant (Asc) and 7th
House Neptune (♆) can be handled with careful deliberation to resolve possible issues with females in
a work setting. Of course, this Protector has several other strategic resources in his amazing *arsenal* to
win over the females in his life to his point of view. He has all the tools he needs to serve as a responsible
Protector and experience the full range of human potential.

Security

The only "security" we can count on is found in our *Inner* Plane.
For greater control of our lives,
we must learn to live on the *Outer* Plane <u>from</u> the Inner Plane.

And – oh, by the way . . .
if at first you feel as though you're "making it up" –
as in the images and messages coming to you,
just *be* with that,
and keep doing "the work."
As Dianne DL says it: "you're not consciously making up something;
it's not like writing a fiction story; it's coming from your Inner self."

You'll receive *signs* soon enough that you're on the right track.

CHAPTER FOUR

PRIOR TO MEETING YOUR ARCHETYPES . . .

Get a sense of their Energy Influences
as a stepping-off point to building a relationship with them.

Find out whether you have Consciousness Resistant Factors (CRFs) pages 22.
Look at the *Keywords for Zodiac Signs and Horoscope Houses* (pages 6-12),
Quick-Reference Keywords for Planets and Luminaries (pages 13-14),
and the *Tarot – Archetype Essences* (pages 45-47),
related to the Sign and planet or luminary (Sun/Moon).

Example

Imagine that Mars is in the 9th House of a birth chart.
The Archetypes for planet Mars ♂ in the Sign of Virgo ♍ are Tower and Hermit, respectively.
You would look for Mars in the *Quick-Reference Keywords for Planets and Luminaries*
and for Virgo and the 9th House in *Keywords for Zodiac Signs and Horoscope Houses*.
You would look for Tower and Hermit in the *Tarot – Archetype Essences*.
These will give you an idea of the Energy Influences and Archetypes of a 9th House Mars in Virgo.

Referring to the Keywords

for the initial meeting with each Archetype
will give you an idea of each Archetype's energy
when you ask your Guide to bring him or her in front of you, and when
you give them permission to become one human-like figure.
Their essence and individual traits mature as your relationship with them grows.

Let's go swimming . . .

Consciousness Resistant Factors
(CRFs)
What are they?

If you have one or more CRFs in your birth chart,
these very *helpful* Archetypes were pushed into the darkness of unconsciousness
when you were born.
They can push you around; they can project your gifts onto others;
or people in the Outer World give you a hard time.

CRFs block your efforts to reach your Center and to have all the good you are meant to experience.

Until you meet and acknowledge and incorporate them into your life,
the other Archetypes cannot function to bring you to full Center.

A circle of hands with your CRFs in your regular meditation
acknowledges their presence within you and allows them to participate in your life.
These Archetypes can then become Consciousness *receptive* Factors (CrFs).

CrFs
open the space to becoming all of who we are.

Do You Have CRFs?

Below, you will find two lists of Consciousness Resistant Factors, one representing CRF Signs in males and the other representing CRF Signs in females. As you become more familiar with oppositions (☍) in astrology, you will notice the lists indicate opposite CRF Signs between male and female. Look at your birth chart for the Sun, Moon, and planets in the Signs indicated in the appropriate column.

If you have one or more CRFs, meet these Archetypes individually the first time, according to their Sign and planet, Sun, or Moon. Later, you will often work <u>separately</u> with them.

See *Tarot – Archetype Essences* (pages 45-47), for a sense of their individual energy.

CRFs in a Male

Sun ☉

Aquarius ♒: Sun and Star
Libra ♎: Sun and Justice

☽ Moon/High Priestess

Capricorn ♑: Old Pan and High Priestess
Scorpio ♏: Death and High Priestess

☿ Mercury/Magician

Sagittarius ♐: Temperance and Magician
Pisces ♓: Moon and Magician
Leo ♌: Strength and Magician

♀ Venus/Empress

Scorpio ♏: Death and Empress
Aries ♈: Emperor and Empress
Virgo ♍: Hermit and Empress

♂ Mars/Tower

Libra ♎: Justice and Tower
Cancer ♋: Chariot and Tower

♃ Jupiter/Wheel of Fortune

Capricorn ♑: Old Pan and Wheel of Fortune
Gemini ♊: Twins and Wheel of Fortune

CRFs in a Female

Sun ☉

Leo ♌: Sun and Strength
Aries ♈: Sun and Emperor

☽ Moon/High Priestess

Cancer ♋: Chariot and High Priestess
Taurus ♉: Hierophant and High Priestess

☿ Mercury/Magician

Gemini ♊: Twins and Magician
Virgo ♍: Hermit and Magician
Aquarius ♒: Star and Magician

♀ Venus/Empress

Taurus ♉: Hierophant and Empress
Libra ♎: Justice and Empress
Pisces ♓: Moon and Empress

♂ Mars/Tower

Aries ♈: Emperor and Tower
Capricorn ♑: Old Pan and Tower

♃ Jupiter/Wheel of Fortune

Cancer ♋: Chariot and Wheel of Fortune
Sagittarius ♐: Temperance and Wheel of Fortune

♄ Saturn/World
Aries ♈ : Emperor and World
Cancer ♋ : Chariot and World

♄ Saturn/World
Libra ♎ : Justice and World
Capricorn ♑ : Old Pan and World

♅ Uranus/Fool
Leo ♌ : Strength and Fool
Taurus ♉ : Hierophant and Fool

♅ Uranus/Fool
Aquarius ♒ : Star and Fool
Scorpio ♏ : Death and Fool

♆ Neptune/Hanged Man
Gemini ♊ : Twins and Hanged Man
Virgo ♍ : Hermit and Hanged Man

♆ Neptune/Hanged Man
Sagittarius ♐ : Temperance and Hanged Man
Pisces ♓ : Moon and Hanged Man

♇ Pluto/Judgment
Taurus ♉ : Hierophant and Judgment
Aquarius ♒ : Star and Judgment

♇ Pluto/Judgment
Scorpio ♏ : Death and Judgment
Leo ♌ : Strength and Judgment

In Regular Meditation

Until you have organized your meditation process (see Template for Daily Meditation page 76),
a digital audio recording and/or writing process will be an invaluable reference.

As you begin regular meditation, immediately after you meet separately with your Guide and Shadows,
ask your Guide to bring your CRFs/CrFs in a circle of hands (format on page 26)
to acknowledge each of them and to balance their energies within you.

This opens the way for full interaction with all the Archetypes.

Let's go swimming . . .

Your Guide

His personality and appearance are shown in
the 9ᵗʰ House of your birth chart
which is his Ascendant.
He represents the expansion of your consciousness.

Your Animal Companion in Your Inner Landscape

The possibilities of the type of animal that comes to you in the Initiation relate to a
planet or luminary in your chart, its placement and Sign.
It seems to be related to our instinctive nature.

After the Initiation, any time you are on the Inner Plane, stay with your Guide and that animal.
Ask your Guide what function your animal may serve.
(Ed tells us more about the animal's presence on pages 111-112 in his book.)

♈ Aries – wolf, ram, lamb
♉ Taurus – cows, pig, bull, boar
♊ Gemini – small bird
♋ Cancer – any animal with a pouch
♌ Leo – lion, large wild cat
♍ Virgo – dog/domesticated protective animal
♎ Libra – dove
♏ Scorpio – reptile animal
♐ Sagittarius – horse
♑ Capricorn – goat, giraffe
♒ Aquarius – large bird
♓ Pisces – water animal
☉ Sun – large feline animal
☽ Moon – cow
☿ Mercury – small, domestic animal
♀ Venus – songbird, parrot, cat, deer,
♂ Mars – animal of prey, hawk
♃ Jupiter – elephant, horse
♄ Saturn – birds of prey, donkey
♅ Uranus – wild game
♆ Neptune – wild animal
♇ Pluto – serpent, skunk, predator bird

Circles of Hands

(Format: see page 26)

We balance the Energy Influences among our Archetypes
and with ourselves and our Guide by doing a circle of hands.
There are separate circles of hands for various purposes.

Your Guide is at the top of the circle, and you would stand to his left.
The pertinent Archetypes stand to your left, completing the circle
to the right of your Guide.
Let your Guide be the one to release the circle
(though you can certainly ask him to do it if you get impatient).

The First Circles

Consciousness Resistant Factors (CRFs)
High Energy Relationships
Archetypes for Moon of the Day
Basic Archetypes (Board of Directors)
Manifestation Archetypes (Signs on/in Houses 2, 5, 8, 11)

Adding On

CRFs
Personal Moon Transit Archetypes
Basic Archetypes (Board of Directors)
Manifestation Archetypes (Signs on/in Houses 2, 5, 8, 11)

Advancing

CRFs
Luminaries and Planet aspecting Archetypes
Archetypes with long-term planet aspects may need a separate circle.
Basic Archetypes (Board of Directors)
Manifestation Archetypes (Signs on/in Houses 2, 5, 8, 11)

A Few Additional Circles:

When you Work on Problems
Negative People (Pages 113-115 in IGM)

Circle of Hands Format

Your Guide
is at the top of the circle, and
you are to his left, with
your Archetypes filling out
the rest of the circle.

The circle of hands is used from the first meeting
of each Archetype and in all subsequent meditation sessions.

Once you have met all of your Archetypes,
use the circle of hands in each meditation session, first
to connect with your CRFs before working with any other Archetypes.
Maintaining this regular connection with your CRFs
will help ensure they do not block your
intentions and the help of your other Archetypes.

In each meditation session, you will meditate with one or more Archetypes.
Ask your Guide to bring each Archetype, and at the conclusion
of your discussion, join hands as shown above.
Feel the energy of the circle, and
let your Guide release hands.

Cleaning Your Aura

In particular, before your IGM Initiation and, thereafter, before each IGM session,
cleaning your aura can open the channel to an invigorated and fresh approach
to meeting and working with your Archetypes.
It is, however, very cleansing at any time.
(You may or may not see your aura right away.)

1. Stand in a quiet state (and room).

2. Brush yourself off without touching yourself – head to toe.

3. Close your eyes, and raise your arms straight overhead (shoulder-width apart).

4. See a cylindrical white light (tinged with is what is likely the color of your own aura); see it go right through your body and out the bottoms of your feet, through the foundation of where you are, and deeper than the roots of any tree you can imagine.

5. Be with this for a few seconds.

6. Now use your hands to encircle your head and begin covering your body with your fresh aura (it may be the same color every time). Circle your head several times, saying, "Please protect me from self-deception, disillusionment, dishonesty, emotional problems, mental illnesses, diseases, the negativity, deceit, and illnesses of others."

7. Continue to cover your body with your fresh aura, bending down all the way to your feet, then "fluff" your aura as you come to an upright position.

8. With your eyes still closed, open your arms wide to allow yourself to feel the exquisite energy of this protection.

Also clean your aura before sleeping to help release pressures.

CHAPTER FIVE

IDENTIFY YOUR ALIEN ENERGY CONSTRUCTS OR PROTECTOR PATTERN

(See also Adept, Alien Energy Constructs, and Protector
in the Appendix of this book and more in Ed's IGM, pages 217-228)

Alien patterns are specific planetary placements and unions
or the absence of planets, Sun, Moon, and Ascendant
in certain zodiacal signs which produce highly specialized individuals.

Adepts have expertise in the area where they do not have
one of the Elements or Qualities for the
Planets, Sun, Moon, and Ascendant.

Protectors have no Alien constructs and have possibilities
of the full range of human potential.

It is not only the Energy Influences of transits that can shape who we are and the respect we have for ourselves and others, but the _Energy Influences_ of who we are can inform our *self*-respect and open possibilities for understanding others at an energetic level, carrying the weight of natural/ automatic respect without the need to "*earn*" respect.

Imagine the difference it can make in our interactions and expectations of one another when everyone knows who they are "energetically" according to whether they have one or more Alien Energy Constructs, Adepts, or is a Protector.

Whether or not one is conscious of being an Alien Power, Alien Vessel, or Alien Instrument, the effects on others around these Aliens take place. The Adept's expertise cannot be applied to their own lives until the Adept is brought into consciousness. Protector energy operates for good or not, depending upon one's awareness, approach in use, and level of humility. Once initiated into the IGM, people can *consciously* make the most of the opportunities they bring to this life experience by working with their Alien Energy Constructs or Adepts in meditation and through transits or, in the case of the Protector, operating with humility for the gift of the full panoply of human potential, understanding, and respect for those with specialized talents from a conscious perspective within the IGM and transits.

Parents of Children Ages 7-13

From a child's birth chart,
learn which Alien Energy Construct or Protector the child is.
Learn and honor the gifts, and
notice when your child is out of balance with that Energy.

Parents can introduce their child to his or her Shadows by age 7.
Shadow playmates can become the silent partners who help a child in one-to-one interactions.

When your child is acting out or otherwise not getting along with siblings at home,
or with siblings at their grandparents' home,
send him or her to another room (or the "kids' room")
for 10 minutes
to talk with their Shadows and
to come out with a better approach to getting along with siblings.

Alien Energy Constructs . . .
Alien Power, Alien Vessel, and Alien Instrument

As you may have already experienced . . .
if <u>your</u> Inner self includes an Alien Energy Construct,
a *"traditional"* or *"conventional"* lifestyle may not work so well for you.

Ask what she or he needs to facilitate
becoming fully conscious within you, and ask where to meet with her or him on a
regular basis to teach you all the mysteries, powers, and abilities
you came into this life experience to use and share in the Outer Plane.

By taking advantage of specialized gifts, which are yours to *borrow*
in this life experience, you are more likely to find peace and joy.
Conversely, you are likely to experience more difficulties
when your gifts are suppressed or resisted.

Female A
Mutual Reception Saturnian Vessel

Female A (see her Chart on page 72). This individual carries the energy of a Mutual Reception Saturnian Vessel with her Moon in Capricorn (☽ ♑) in the 2nd House and Saturn in Cancer (♄ ♋) in her 8th House. As such, her 2nd House Moon functions in both the 2nd House and 8th House; her Saturn functions in both the 8th House and 2nd House. Her talents and abilities can lie quiescent as her Saturnian Vessel pushes from within for greater awakening and use at some later point in life. Awakened, she is uniquely gifted to bring constructive purpose and a stabilizing influence to those in her environment. She is a "tester" of humanity at the same time she is a "guardian" of humanity.

This individual is fully engaged in life with the depth-perspective of her personal IGM growth. Even with many requests for her assistance personally and professionally, she continues to grow within IGM. As she says, "there are no more black holes" in understanding how to function as herself on the Outer Plane. She totally understands that to fully embrace her gift as a way of life, she cannot avoid doing regular meditation. She cannot afford to be unaware of abilities emanating from this Alien, as they would otherwise be projected outside of her. She would then be more vulnerable to work-a-holism, addictions, despair, anxiety, and fear, among other imbalances in her actions, health, and communications.

Female B
Uranian Power and Earth Adept

Female B Chart is on page 114. This individual is a Uranian Power and Earth Adept. She is a master of empathy, has highly unique qualities, is altruistic, and has the genius of multi-level awareness. As a Uranian Power, along with having the opportunity to ensure that natural law on Earth Plane conforms to Universal law when there are major changes in her environment, she is innately gifted in creating projects, or "seeing" ideas, years ahead of human understanding. Resistance to using these gifts can manifest in coldness toward others, electrical overcharges in her body, and, among other inconvenient maladies, acute nervousness.

As an Earth Adept, as long as this Archetype is conscious within her, this Uranian Power also shows expertise in all Earth Plane life areas, including but not limited to stability, work methods, career matters, worldly achievement, structure, money, food, and health, as well as the ability to help others in these areas.

Female C

Protector

Female C Chart is on page 40. This extremely intelligent, well-traveled, free-spirited Protector takes full advantage of every life opportunity within her highly individualistic lifestyle and priorities. She recognizes her responsibility as a Protector, without attempting to control her environment at the expense of others. While she is not intimidated by the Alien Energy Constructs or Adepts, she also does not attempt to weaken acceptance of their talents by others. Where the destinies of many people are controlled by others, Female C is in control of her own destiny and acts with full integrity on the Inner Plane with acceptable results on the Outer Plane when life isn't kind. Her Shadows have truly become her conscious, equal partners, and the communication with all her Archetypes is regular and spirited.

Female D

Protector

Female D Chart is on page 35. This Protector was surprised at her ability to experience the IGM Initiation with such ease and depth (Protectors can access the IGM easier than the Aliens). She is also blessed to understand and fit into any cultural or social milieu, with an added ability to immediately make anyone feel comfortable in her presence. She is mature beyond her years and, with a conscious Pluto/Judgment, can use her particular genius as an agent of change, exerting her considerable influence for the good of all.

She particularly enjoys the New Moon Cycle Planning and Goal Setting ritual each month – the tactility of working with her Tarot cards and, in the process, grinning at the truthfulness/consistency of their Energy Influences.

FEMALE D CHART

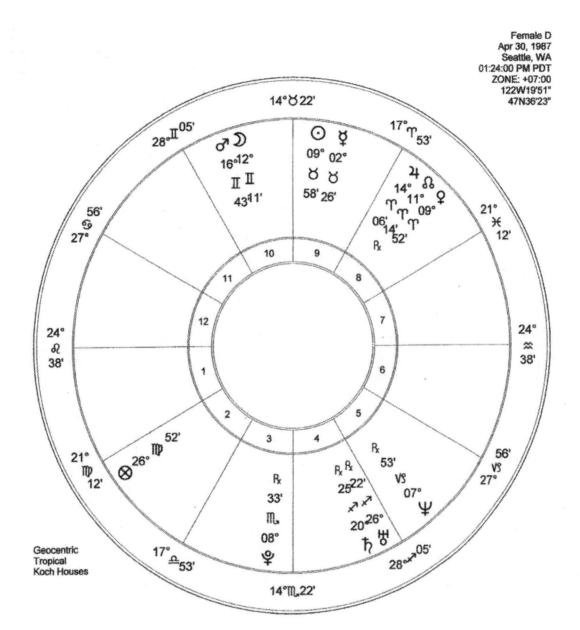

Female D
Apr 30, 1987
Seattle, WA
01:24:00 PM PDT
ZONE: +07:00
122W19'51"
47N36'23"

Geocentric
Tropical
Koch Houses

FEMALE E CHART

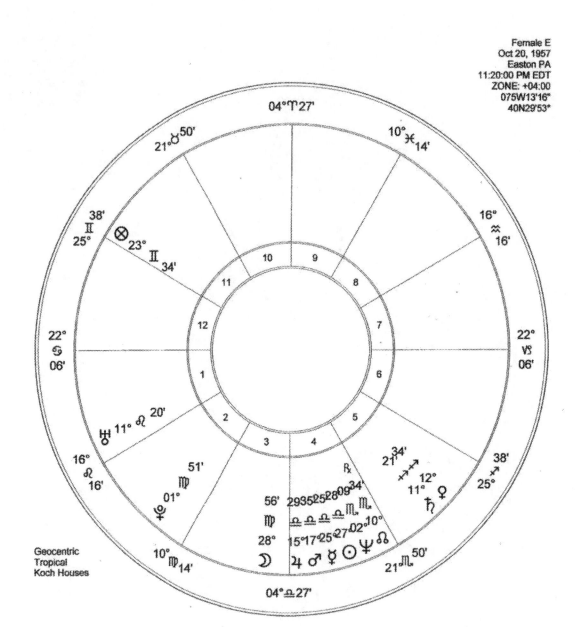

Female E
Oct 20, 1957
Easton PA
11:20:00 PM EDT
ZONE: +04:00
075W13'16"
40N29'53"

Geocentric
Tropical
Koch Houses

Female E
Neptunian Power
with Uranian Instrument Influence

Female E, whose Chart is on the opposite page, is a clairvoyant/claircognizant individual who now takes her ability seriously. She is a Neptunian Power, who also operates as a Uranian Instrument, is a genius without Consciousness Resistant Factors to block her purity. She is genuinely altruistic, and her powerful influence crosses cultural and class boundaries with a refined naturalness and grace.

She brings a futuristic and realistic mindset to community involvement with the education and experience to influence thinking of cohorts. She also contributes considerable business acumen and psychic ability to assist those desirous of starting new ventures. With the ability to make herself visible or seemingly *invisible*, this individual moves through life with an air of compassionate lightness of being and brings greater understanding to serious issues and sociability where it is absent.

This Neptunian/Uranian stays aware of transits and stays true to her iconoclastic individuality in planning around them with a light touch. She uses her "crew" (Guide and Shadows) to advise her in a pinch. She'll say words to this effect, "Okay, *(name of Guide)*, let's get this figured out." She invariably receives a message about the immediate next step – or which Archetype will help her move an issue to resolution and the correct action.

CHAPTER SIX

INITIATION INTO THE INNER GUIDE MEDITATION

Suggested Initiation Outline Template
(Adapted from and to be used with the IGM book, pages 53-63)

Date:
Cave (Description):
Animal Companion on the Inner Plane (Description and Name):
Guide (Description and Name):

Do "First Questions" to each Archetype (see page 39),
and write or otherwise record their appearance, clothing, and names.

Sun: _____
Consciousness Resistant Factors (CRFs): _____
Solar Center Construct or Power Alien:

Sun and its Sign and planets/Moon which are conjunct = Male figure

Alien Energy Construct (Personal Moon conjunct one or more planets and the Sign):
(Feminine Receptive Principle, Lunar Construct and Inner Mother):
High Priestess + Planet(s) + Sign = Female figure
Or:
If there are no Alien Constructs, the individual is a "Protector,"
and
the Lunar Construct/Inner Mother is comprised of the
High Priestess and the Sign of the individual's Personal Moon = Female figure

Chart Ruler: Sign on the Ascendant/1st House (and a Co-Ruler if the Sign on the ASC is in the last 2 degrees, in which case, the Ruler of the Sign filling most of the 1st House is the other Co-Ruler)

Basic Archetypes (Board of Directors/Advisors) (see IGM, page 215)
Sun and its Sign; Planets in Rulership; and Final Dispositors

Shadows: 1 Male and 1 Female. (Unless you have Gemini or Sagittarius on the 1st House cusp, which is the Ascendant or Rising Sign ; then, you will have 4 Shadows: 2 males and 2 females)
Meeting Place with your Guide: (Where is it in your Inner Landscape? Write a description of the setting.)
Name of your Guide (if he wasn't forthcoming at the beginning of your initiation): _____

Return to the cave entrance with your animal; say goodbye,
and go through your cave to the Outer Plane.

(Once you're in the Outer Plane, wriggle your toes, and feel your feet on the floor or ground.)

First Questions When Meeting Each Archetype with Your Guide
(Adapted from page 211 of Ed's book)

1. What do you need from me and from my life to work with me and be my friend?

2. What gift (symbolic object) do you have for me that I need from you?

3. Ask for an interpretation of the talent or ability it represents.

4. Ask about its powers.

5. Ask about its uses as a tool.

6. Confirm with your Guide that you should accept this gift.

7. If the answer is yes, ask the Archetype where in your body it is to be carried and absorbed as a reminder of its essence within you.

8. Ask the Archetype to acquaint you with its sphere of influence on your Inner Plane and where it lives in your Inner Landscape.

9. Ask the Archetype what his or her relevance is in your Outer world (beyond the *Tarot – Archetype Essences* pages 45-47).

10. Ask what she or he creates and sustains in your Outer world (beyond the *Sign*, planet, luminary, and placement in your chart).

11. Ask how you can change and/or what you need to change so the Archetype can evolve into his or her most spiritual form within you.

FEMALE C CHART

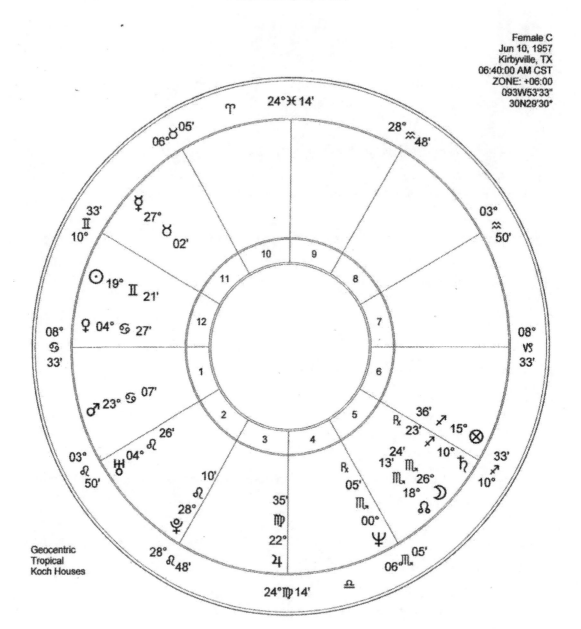

Female C
Jun 10, 1957
Kirbyville, TX
06:40:00 AM CST
ZONE: +06:00
093W53'33"
30N29'30"

Geocentric
Tropical
Koch Houses

INNER GUIDE MEDITATION WORKSHEET FOR FEMALE C

HIGH ENERGY RELATIONSHIPS
(They don't always work easily together):
High Priestess and Judgment
Death and Strength
High Priestess and Magician
Death and Hierophant
Fool and Hanged Man
Temperance and Death
Magician and Judgment
Hierophant and Strength
Moon and Hermit
Moon and Wheel of Fortune
Moon and Sun
Moon and Duality
Sun and Wheel of Fortune
Duality and Hermit

CHECK THE UNION BETWEEN
(These usually work well together):
High Priestess and Wheel of Fortune
Death and Hermit
Sun and Tower
Duality and Chariot
Sun and Judgment
Duality and Strength
Sun and World
Duality and Temperance
Moon and Magician
Moon and Hierophant
Empress and Fool
Tower and Wheel of Fortune
Chariot and Hermit

BASIC ARCHETYPES - Board of Directors
**(Memorize their seating along with your Guide,
You, and your Shadows, and discuss life questions and
projects with them so you have a vote and greater
control over potentially life-altering events):**

Sun	Duality
Mercury	Hierophant
Empress	Chariot
High Priestess	Death
Judgment	Strength

Energy Influences
www.moonlinks.net
moonlinks@earthlink.net

INNER GUIDE MEDITATION WORKSHEET FOR FEMALE C

First Questions to Archetypes (with your Guide):
What do you need from me and from my life to work
with me and be my friend? What gift do you have for
me that I need from you? (This will be a symbolic
object. Ask for an interpretation as to what talent or
ability it represents, its powers and uses as a tool, and
where in your body it is to be carried and absorbed.)

**CIRCLES OF HANDS WITH (including your Guide, You,
and your Shadows):**
Basic Archetypes/Board of Directors
Empress, Tower, and Chariot
Magician, S. Node, and Hierophant
Fool, Judgment, and Strength
Hanged Man, N.Node, High Priestess, Death,
    Chiron and Star
Sun, Duality, Wheel of Fortune, Hermit, World,
    Part of Fortune, Temperance, and Moon
High Energy Pairs and Union Pairs

SOLAR CENTER CONSTRUCT: (Masculine-Creative
Principle, Higher Self, Solar Center, and Primary
Purpose) =
    Male Figure
    Sun + Duality (2 male figures)

PROTECTOR PATTERN

LUNAR CONSTRUCT: (Feminine-Receptive Principle,
Inner Mother) =
    Female Figure
    High Priestess + Death

FIXED T-CROSS ENERGY BALANCING CONSTRUCT:

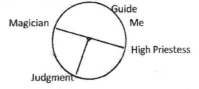

CONSCIOUSNESS RESISTANT FACTORS
(When you were born, they were pushed into the
darkness of consciousness):
    Judgment   Strength

Worksheet Template Articulation

When first meeting your Archetypes, follow the Worksheet guidelines
with additional information about the First Questions to be found on page 39.
Always give them <u>permission</u> to respond to you.
If you are frightened or uncomfortable with an Archetype,
say so, and ask your Guide what you can do to open the space for loving communication.

These Archetypes will, of course, be different in everyone's chart;
however, identifying their Energy Influence is the same, i.e., ☌ ✶ □ △ ⚻ ☍ .

High Energy Relationships: These are pairs of Tarot Archetypes representing great positive potential through various tests and conflicts in one's birth chart. Inasmuch as transits trigger these relationships on a regular basis, you will be able to work with these Archetypes in meditation. Let them know you're aware of the problems and pain they can cause you, and you will do your part to heal their relationships within you, so life is more manageable on the Outer Plane. Ask what they need from each other and from you to work together for the good of all and in your best interests.

Your Archetypes may want you to *stop* doing something,
but they will never suggest that you bring harm to any living thing,
nor will they ask you to do something impossibly difficult.

After the initial meeting, you will be able to see ahead of time on your Table of Basic Aspects (page 73)
and Astrological Calendar when they are likely to cause a problem through transits.
You will be able to *plan* ahead when you see the
Moon sign, Sun, or planets in either of the two signs of each pair.

They are based on the following Energy Influences:

90° □ (Square) (within 7° +/-): an aspect which brings ongoing tests and challenges to be acknowledged and creatively addressed with your Archetypes in meditation.

150° ⚻ (Quincunx/Inconjunct) (within 3° +/-): an aspect which brings annoying "opportunities" to adjust one's behavior, expectations, and/or actions to cooperate with the inevitable in your "best interest."

180° ☍ (Opposition) (within 7° +/-): an aspect which brings ongoing climactic events (conflicts with both plus and minus results) to be acknowledged and proactively addressed with your Archetypes in meditation. (Also see *Healing the Relationship between Opposites*, Chapter Nine, page 61.)

Check the Union between the following aspecting Archetypes to make sure each pair is working well together – as they usually are. In your initial meeting with these Archetypes, ask how you can be a catalyst for their intrinsic harmony. After your initial meeting, they will come up in transits, and you will be able to plan how best to use their Energy Influences by looking ahead of time on your Table of Basic Aspects and an Astrological Calendar. Understand that they can get pushed into acting separately and, therefore, not in your best interest, so it's beneficial to check in with them on a regular basis, especially if the pairs don't come up in your transits when you see the Moon sign, Sun, or planets.

They are based upon the following Energy Influences:

0° ☌ (Conjunction) (within 7° +/-): an aspect representing "union." Whether or not it is a compatible union depends on which Signs and luminaries and/or planets are conjunct. So, on the one hand, we look for the compatible union, while on the other hand, we work with our Archetypes to bring favorable energy to ease any incompatibility.

60° ⚹ (Sextile) (within 5° +/-): an aspect that brings opportunity requiring action. On the one hand, they can ease tension in one's day; on the other they can sap one's drive to accomplish something worthwhile unless consciously activated through meditation with your Archetypes. So, the initial meeting is important to get the ball rolling; thereafter, take advantage of the opportunities the sextile brings through transits.

120° △ (Trine) (within 7° +/-): an aspect of relative *ease* that cannot be taken for granted. For example, there may be a wonderful trine between two planets that indicates "no problem – piece of cake" which, when left dangling, can actually create unnecessary issues! The key is to look ahead, and <u>plan</u> with your Archetypes how to *use* this aspect of *ease*. In some cases, the trine automatically brings greater flow to one's activities and interactions; just don't count on it without helping to make it happen.

After each discussion with your Archetypes in mediation,
use circles of hands to balance their energies with yours.

CHAPTER SEVEN

MEETING YOUR REMAINING ARCHETYPES

Use the Meditation for the Initial Meeting of Archetypes (page 48)
and First Questions (page 39) and Closing (page 48)
With your birth chart in front of you, start at the 1st House, and list the Archetypes (Signs, planets, luminaries, North Node, South Node, and Chiron) you did not meet when you were initiated or when you initiated yourself using *The Inner Guide Meditation* book.

Your North Node ☊ and South Node ☋ as Archetypes

The North and South Lunar Nodes form the nodal axis from the intersection of the Ecliptic and the Moon's orbit in an angular relationship to the Sun. The North Node represents where the Moon crosses the Ecliptic going North. It is often said to be our "destiny factor," and where our greatest fulfillment lies. It is also the hardest path to follow. The South Node is directly opposite the North Node and represents where the Moon crosses the Ecliptic going South. It is the easiest path to take, because it's what we already know, and can lead to our downfall if not balanced with the efforts necessary through the North Node.

In the Inner Guide Meditation, our North and South Node Archetypes are formed with the Sign in which they are found. We ask our Guide to bring the North Node and its Sign before us and give them permission to dissolve through an oval of light and condense into one human-like figure. Write its appearance, and ask its name. The same process is used to form the South Node Archetype.

In a circle of hands with your Guide, balance the energies of the North and South Node figures for greater ease in reaching the fulfillment offered by the North Node in the House where it is posited. In transits (planets and luminaries in the sky connecting with your personal planets and luminaries on a daily basis), you will then include these Archetypes when they are aspecting/connecting with your planets and/or luminaries. Thank them, and let your Guide be the first one to release hands in the circle.

Chiron ⚷ as an Archetype

Chiron was discovered in 1977 and dubbed a planetoid, being too large for an asteroid and small for a planet. It was named after the Greek mythological Centaur. To paraphrase Melanie Reinhart's description, in *Chiron and the Healing Journey* (pages 3-6), Chiron was discovered between Saturn and Uranus, and its archetypal pattern thus suggests the paradox in human terms of limitless inspiration and one's fixed psyche and suffering, based upon the birth chart, familial influences, and societal conditioning, as well as karmic inheritance. It represents "a spirit of philosophical independence, compassion in the face of our suffering, and an ongoing process of learning to trust the Inner Teacher or Guide."

Chiron represents a "wound," and we all carry one. We can achieve positive, conscious goals where he lives in our birth chart when we acknowledge his presence as a wounded healer in us and, in meditations, learn the gifts he brings because of, or in spite of, the wound.

Ask your Guide to bring Chiron and the Archetype of his Sign to meet you, and give them permission to dissolve through an oval of light and condense into his highest human-like form at this time. Make note of his appearance and ask his name. Join in a circle of hands to begin balancing his energy within you. Thank him, and let your Guide break the circle.

Tarot–Archetype Essences
. . . if we ask our Archetypes for assistance – and if they are <u>Un</u>blocked and Conscious.

(These are partially adapted from my notes as taken in Laurel Kahaner's Tarot classes in the 1990s.)
Tarot for Your Self by Mary K. Greer is an exceptional added resource.

0 – **Fool** (Uranus ♅) (Aleph): harbinger of radical change; free spirit; being open to the unexpected with no sense of worry or fear; trusting life and yourself to take a leap without knowing where your feet will land; being unable to prepare for the obstacles or figure it all out – the ultimate intelligent risk-taker.

1 – **Magician** (Mercury ☿) (Beth): power of the mind to accurately and responsibly communicate on the Inner Plane to make something real out of the possibilities in the Outer World; the result of the leap of faith taken by the Fool; being open to connecting with power; have enough self-love to focus on one thing at a time and not give away all your power; manipulative trickster, playfulness.

2 – **High Priestess** (personal Moon ☽) (Gimel): the uniting intelligence; perfect memory; she knows everything that has happened or will happen; wise, deep channel of consciousness; she unites you with the object of your focus; she likes to "sit with a thought" – wait a minute; thinking by comparison.

3 – **Empress** (Venus ♀) (Daleth): the door opener to endless creativity; she directs your creative imagination – stretch yourself; exert your power with a loving hand; have an open and sympathetic heart; build happy and stable relationships; deep unfoldment, expansion; a desire to "give birth" to something remarkable.

4 – **Emperor** (Aries ♈) (He): creating a stable situation from which to function and take action; getting down to basics; the light by which you want to live your life; taking reasonable risks; confidence; assertion; following through with tenacity.

5 – **Hierophant/High Priest** (Taurus ♉) (Vau): helps us listen on the Inner Plane; strive to live from intuition; get out of the way so you can hear your Archetypes; sense of touch; the gentleness of music will help you to truly "let go"; used well, he can show you how to stand up for yourself against bullying.

6 – **Duality/Twins** (Gemini ♊) (Zain): discriminating/choosing between two of anything; risking choice; asking the conscious and subconscious to connect with your higher self; getting clarity, and choosing only extraordinary relationships that mirror your self-worth; not reflecting back; finding bliss in little things; you may be focusing too much on the surface.

7 – **Chariot** (Cancer ♋) (Cheth): profound transformation; victory through knowing the boundaries; the card of those who achieve greatness; Fool is the charioteer; deciding what your goal is and how many hours a day you are going to give it; some commitment to Spirit has paid off; a battle of sheer will has been won; living life with authority; exerting willpower over your dual nature; taking care of the physical body without expending too much energy; concentrating on external affairs.

8 – **Strength** (Leo ♌) (Teth): strength from creativity and the love and support of others; having enough self-love to manage your life well; she tames with an enlightened spiritual touch; conquering your natural fears and harnessing the infinite powers of your spirit; desiring strongly, and giving the result to Spirit; with gentleness, accomplishing what force cannot. When your Outer reality creates distraction, go immediately to your Inner reality to *recreate* your <u>own</u> Outer reality! Constantly recreate yourself by constantly taking in your *Essential Energy* at your brain pool.

9 – **Hermit** (Virgo ♍) (Yod): looking broader; solitude is needed so you are not distracted from looking into your soul; commitment to follow your soul's path; the integration of your experiences; analyzing in a positive way what's not working; Hermit lights the path of your direction; a feeling exquisite beyond belief; being patient, cautious, quiet, and discreet; allowing yourself to be healed.

10 – **Wheel of Fortune** (Jupiter ♃) (Kaph): she/he helps you center yourself and rewards the intelligence of those who seek; thinking ahead and considering your actions; lessons from the past; taking responsibility; letting all your talents show; grasping the cycle you're in; centering yourself; being open to unexpected luck, opportunity, and expansion.

11 – **Justice** (Libra ♎) (Lamed): cutting away with the swiftness of a sword that which is no longer necessary to maintain equilibrium; not a gentle card; mercy and severity; no punishment implied; what is your purpose right now? what is required to regain your equilibrium?; having faith that justice will prevail; fairness; staying faithful to that which is connected to the Fool.

12 – **Hanged Man** (Neptune ♆) (Mem): can cause an ecstatic feeling; looking at things from the opposite point of view; not making decisions right now because you don't yet have all the information needed; listening to your Inner Guides; surrendering to your Inner self – getting out of your own way; ceasing or minimizing motion/activity.

13 – **Death** (Scorpio ♏) (Nun): getting down to basics of deep transformation; letting go of one thing to gain another; regeneration; imaginative intelligence; fantasizing wisely; imagining yourself closer and closer to Center; this is where things currently are.

14 – **Temperance** (Sagittarius ♐) (Samekh): experimenting, tempering/blending opposing factors; using moderation as you shoot higher than you think you can while maintaining harmony with practical considerations and natural law; pushing it through; learning to blend opposing factors; Temperance strengthens to move the energy; having an ongoing conversation with your Inner Guide; asking, "How do I combine the energy toward what my goal is – toward a beneficial synthesis of the spiritual and material worlds?"

15 – **Old Pan/Devil** (Capricorn ♑) (Ayin): working with your Shadows – asking: "Where am I not seeing deeply enough?" Looking at what's stuck; where are you limiting yourself? Seeking to radically alter your thoughts. Blocks will be removed; understanding your limitations; *playing* more; sharing humor; being careful of over-materialism; may be taking yourself too seriously; being tolerant and compassionate toward yourself; asking to see beyond the veil of truth; being content with *self*-approval.

16 – **Tower** (Mars ♂) (Peh): exciting intelligence; like a bolt of lightning, Tower cracks you out of restrictions; it represents conflicts inherent in your behavior when you attempt to structure your life by convention; the lightning causes you to change and live your chosen way; illusions are shattered; radical restructuring; instantaneous profound change – when something is done, it's done! Abandoning that which is not truly your own; breaking down barriers; other change will come, but you'll go on – sublime destruction.

17 – **Star** (Aquarius ♒) (Tzaddi): gentle, life-giving energy; healing revelations to questions we ask; infinite inspiration; individuality; good mental health; asking to participate; everything is really clear; an exquisite time; getting your wish; think about what has come to light.

18 – **Moon** (Pisces ♓) (Qoph): intelligence of the physical body; feel a deeper relationship with your body; emergence of the repressed; be willing to look at whether you're deceiving yourself; ask for a finer vehicle to be a receptacle of change; give your mind suggestions before you sleep.

19 – **Sun** (Leo ☉) (not to be confused with your personal Sun Sign) (Resh): celebrating the playfulness of spirit; arrival; showing the Outer World who you are (the object is to reflect the power of your Inner World); a turn in the journey to Self; blessings, show gratitude; show what you *honor* by giving it your time and energy; let the world feel your warmth.

20 – **Judgment** (Pluto ♇) (Shin): living at the next level of consciousness; the willingness to do the Inner work, which brings irrevocable change/transformation; living in the world and out of it at the same time; making a judgment; reaching a logical conclusion; cooperating with the inevitable; it's time for an important change; listening to your Inner Guide and your Archetypes ends Self-Judgment and begins Self-Definition.

21 – **World** (Saturn ♄) (Tau): completing a cycle; knowing who you are; going within and finding your own harmony; self-mastery, oneness of self and nature; making sure of your direction; dancing on your limitations; balancing inner harmony with skills; establishing yourself in your rightful place as an expression of your Inner and Outer harmony; taking responsibility; realization of a long-sought-after goal; sense of satisfaction; success, harmony, and triumph; being ready to be born again as the Fool.

Meditation for Initial Meeting of Remaining Archetypes
(after Initiation into the IGM)

Enter your cave without watching yourself.
- Feel your feet on the ground and the air around you.

Go out of the doorway to your left, and your Protective Animal will be waiting at that aperture.
- Acknowledge the animal and tell it to take you to your Inner Guide (always be with the animal and your Guide on the Inner Plane).

Follow, without meandering or being distracted, and go to the location where you meet your Guide.

In each sitting, ask your Guide to individually bring each Archetype you haven't yet met.
- For indications of all basic Energy Influences of the Archetypes, see Tarot-Archetype Essences (page 45-47).

Confirm with your Guide that this figure is a true Archetype guide.
- If not, ask your Guide to bring the true Archetype.

Ask the First Questions (page 39) when the true Archetype is in front of you and your Guide.

Upon completion, thank each of them, give them a hug, and say goodbye for now.

With CRFs: Ask these Archetypes to join hands, forming a circle with you and your Guide. Be in the circle, not *watching* it, and feel the energy of this group. Give them permission to balance their energies among each other and with you. Notice how this affects you. Your Guide will break the circle once the energy is flowing.

Either use a digital audio recorder to remember descriptions of your Archetypes, or write them on the description template (page 49).

Closing
Thank your Guide, and if you two are finished working together for now,
have your animal lead you back to the cave entrance,
say goodbye, and
go through your cave
to come back into your Outer World.

(Wriggle your toes, and feel the floor or ground under your feet.)

REMEMBERING YOUR ARCHETYPES

TABLE FORMAT

House & Sign	Archetype for Sign	Appearance and Ethnicity	Gift and Placement	Name of Archetype	Ruler /Planet	Archetype for Ruler/ Planet
1						
2						
3						
4						
5						
6						
7						
8						
9						
10						
11						
12						

Your Archetypes help you live in your own skin . . .
Your Archetypes have your back . . .
You want more, better, "good-er?"
Ask your Guide to help you more clearly define what that means.

Just Get out of the Way!

If this is a new way of living for you,
allow time for your brain to be rewired to follow your blueprint,
to create a time shift to the transition, and emerge regenerated and empowered.

Wake up and become <u>all</u> of yourself!

Let's go swimming . . .

Chapter Eight

MEDITATING OUR WAY TO GREATER FULFILLMENT

Living life as if your life <u>depends</u> on it!
Leaving no loose ends!

Intention
(Adapted from **est** [Erhard Seminar Training] workshops in the 1980s)

Align your intention with the Universe <u>first</u> –
with the group in which you are participating, second.

In a group, listen for the "intentions" of others.
If they're the same as yours, and members are known for keeping their word,
the group effort will likely be successful.

When you feel overwhelmed with so much to squeeze into a little space of time,
always get back to your
<u>Intention</u>!

That aligns your actions with your priorities.
Then, if you run out of time to do "everything,"
you will have at least alleviated feeling overwhelmed
and will have followed your priorities.

What you *intend* is what works!
Just like keeping your word or otherwise responsibly handling that,
by informing all parties, and modifying an agreement.
It just works.

Take the ultimate *get-away* <u>every</u> day!
Meditate in your <u>Inner</u> Landscape.

Preparing for Your Inner Guide Meditation Sessions

Tools Needed:

- *The Inner Guide Meditation, A Spiritual Technology for the 21st Century* by Edwin C. Steinbrecher, Revised 6th Edition, 2nd Printing 1989
- *Book of Changes and the Unchanging Truth* by Taoist Master Ni, Hua Ching (or another I Ching book, if you prefer)
- The Inner Guide Meditation Barometer Chart (page 112)
- Your astrological birth chart (preferably using the Koch House System), based upon your birth certificate* data or other specific birth documentation
- IGM Worksheet (based on your birth chart) adapted in this book on page 41 from the worksheet on page 211 of *The Inner Guide Meditation*
- Tarot cards (see "Your Personal Tarot Deck" on page 55)
- Special bag for your Tarot cards
- Special cloth to use when spreading your Tarot cards
- Astrological Calendar (with Moon Signs, Void of Course Moon dates and times, and ephemeris of dates and Sign degrees of planets and luminaries). The Jim Maynard *Celestial Guide* and/or the *Pocket Astrologer* are suggested.
- Table of Moon Transits to your Birth Chart (page 73)
- Tarot-Archetype Essences (page 45-47), Some Keywords of Zodiac Signs and Horoscope Houses (page 6-12), and Quick-Reference Keywords for Planets and Luminaries (page 13-14)
- Zodiac Sign Goals and Goal Houses (page 150)
- Good Mother Messages (page 173)
- Plain paper (8½ x 11) for meditation notes
- Tabbed folders and/or binder with dividers (or digital recorder for archiving early meditations)

*If the time of your birth is not on your birth certificate, contact the Department of Vital Statistics in the County Seat of the State in which you were born. Request a "Vault Copy" of your birth certificate with the time of birth included. If your birth certificate is ultimately unavailable, a Professional Astrologer can prepare a Rectified Birth Chart for you.

Your Personal Tarot Deck

As you may know, working with Tarot takes us to our subconscious mind. Tarot card Energy Influences represent the essences (though not images) of our personal Archetypes. In this book, they are also used for New Moon Cycle planning and goal setting, as well as for the Good Mother messages.

When purchasing a full deck (Major and Minor Arcana cards), select the deck according to the favorite Major Arcana images you see in a deck for your Sun Sign Archetype, also the Sun card, the High Priestess, your Moon Sign Archetype, your Ascendant Sign Archetype, and the card for the planet or luminary ruling your Ascendant). The energy of the image depicted by the image of the chosen cards often assists us in connecting with our own Archetypes on the Inner Plane. (Sign Rulers are found on the Zodiac list, page 87. Tarot-Archetype Essences are found on pages 45-47.)

To honor the connection with the selected deck, many people keep it in a special pouch and use a special cloth under the cards when spreading them. Out of respect (as taught by Laurel Kahaner), we don't "shuffle" the cards as we might a playing-card deck. Instead, one way is to hold the deck in one hand, and use the other hand to lift out several cards at a time, dropping them back into a different part of the rest of the deck, repeated three times to put our personal energy into the deck (a process to be used also after someone else uses our deck).

Use the Major Arcana to ask which Archetype will take you deeper into a new deck, and leave the card drawn out for a few days to ponder its depths. (Tarot Archetype Essences on pages 45-47 may be useful in this regard, as will be the book *Tarot for Your Self* by Mary K. Greer.)

THE List
Daily Do for IGM

In a binder or folder, these are the basic IGM session sheets you will want to create and include over time, with the objective of covering all your meditation bases in the shortest amount of time, as necessary for your schedule. Each IGM begins with entering your cave and exiting through an aperture to the left to your Inner Landscape to greet your protective animal. Instruct it to take you to your Inner Guide at the meeting place previously selected by your Guide in your Initiation.

Stages of meditation for these steps are self-determined; however, the basic steps below include:

1-5   7-9   13-16 and 18

1. Basic specific talking points for meeting with your Guide (Chapter Ten, page 76, #4).
2. Your Template pages with current date and Moon Phase for meeting with your Guide (page 66).
3. The basic specific talking points for checking in with your Shadows (page 76, #5).
4. Circle of Hands drawing with specific notes acknowledging your CRFs (page 77, #7).
5. Circle of Hands drawing with notes for connecting with your Board of Directors (page 77, #9).
6. Write a reminder page to do your personal I Chings with your Board present.
7. Sign-specific Daily Moon Meditation notes (including aspects/connections) with the Moon Archetype of the day (page 77, #8).
8. Good Mother Messages from your Inner Mother (Lunar Construct) (page 173).
9. Basic specific talking points for greeting your Inner Mother.
10. *Do Daily with Genius* specific talking points and circle of hands with Quintile Archetypes (page 79).
11. Aspirations from the Archetype for current year (page 154).
12. Special circle of hands drawing and notes for connecting with Archetypes of the current Total Solar Eclipse.
13. Current list visualizing what you want to manifest before leaving this life experience. Specify the five most urgent goals (page 147).
14. Goals template (page 149).
15. Circle of Hands drawing with your Manifestation Archetypes from Houses 2, 5, 8, and 11, and a note asking for what you need to make it happen (page 147).
16. Write and put in a reminder note to walk with your Inner Guide, animal, and Shadows through your Inner Landscape up to the home of your Solar Center Construct to acknowledge current transits with your Archetypes.
17. Write transit aspect notes with dates for Sun and planets to make sure you're on purpose using ephemeris and keywords.
18. Your *brain pool* circle of hands after you've caught up with Archetypes for the current IGM session before *going swimming* (page 77, #12).

Scheduling Your Meditations
Early morning is the most important time of day
and should be respected as sacred time
in which to be peaceful
in order not to violate the energy
of the entire day.
Li Hexagram #30, Line 1

Allow the time you can each day.
Do it for 10 to 15 minutes a day, and write what you get.
Do it for 10 to 15 minutes more, and you'll get more.
Do it another 10 to 15 minutes, and you'll get the truth.

For best results,
meditate at approximately the same time every day.
Early morning prepares you for the day's challenges and opportunities
with the greatest support from the transiting Energy Influences.

Clean your Aura, first.
Treasure the time with your Archetypes.
Say their names when working with them.
They help you open the day and clear and close it with an "after-party"
to use for adding comments to your morning meditation notes.

When time is short, connect with your Guide,
the Moon Archetype of the day, your CRFs, and your Shadows.
Ask them to stay with you and to
advise you throughout the day.

When "weird" things come up or happen in meditation,
STOP!
Check it out . . .
Nothing happens by coincidence.
Ed

Be Skeptical . . . It's Healthy!

Be skeptical about the advice coming through your Archetypes,
because your ego may not be seeing their negative side;
for example, with respect to psychic hits or "healing" suggestions.

Red Flags

Being out of body;
Being distracted.
Getting total agreement to everything you say.
If you aren't feeling the energy coming through the circle of hands,
it may be that you are hearing what you want to hear.

When the Archetype from your *Good Mother Messages* (page 173) stops you
from doing something, pay attention!
She is saying "no" for a reason.

Remedies

Ask your Guide to show you how to get grounded.
Confirm the advice you receive through an I Ching question/toss (pages 134-137). . . .
Ask: *How can I be sure of the advice received in my meditation with regard to . . .?*
The hexagram will speak directly to the question.
In your circle of hands, feel the texture, warmth, and size of the hands being held, and
notice how the ground feels beneath your feet.

CHAPTER NINE

FROM THE BEGINNING...

Healing the Relationship between Opposites (☍)

In subsequent meditation sessions, after having met all your Archetypes, do a circle of hands (page 25) with one or more of the following pairs of Archetypes who are in natural opposition to one another (☍ = 180° apart). These Archetypes are in everyone's birth chart and, along with other High Energy Relationship Archetypes; for example, those who are in a 90° square (□) to one another, bring the greatest pain. If they are also CRFs, you will have already met them. For the general Energy Influences, see the *Some Keywords for Zodiac Signs and Horoscope* Houses (page 6-12).

In our early meditation sessions, it is important to balance the energy between these Archetypes. Explain to them, in your meditation format, that they can bring trouble and defeat or they can bring positive energy to be directed into the specific House where they reside in your birth chart. Ask them what they need from each other and from you to shift suffering and pain to helpful positive energy.

In the circle of hands, ask your Guide to balance energies within them and within you. Let him be the first one to release hands. Thank them, and let them go for now. You will be working with them every month during your Daily Moon Meditations and also as you advance in transit meditations.

♈ Aries and Libra ♎
Emperor and Justice

♉ Taurus and Scorpio ♏
Hierophant and Death

♊ Gemini and Sagittarius ♐
Duality and Temperance

♋ Cancer and Capricorn ♑
Chariot and Old Pan

♌ Leo and Aquarius ♒
Strength and Star

♍ Virgo and Pisces ♓
Hermit and Moon

Look at your birth chart for planet and luminary oppositions (☍) in these Signs.
You will want to be aware of those opposing Archetypes,
acknowledge them, and use the above process to gain their cooperation.

Ask your Guide:
"How do I wake up and become all of myself?"

Moon Meditations

You may wish to begin daily Moon Meditation sessions with just the Moon Archetype of the day. The *Table for Remembering Your Archetypes* (page 49) will be useful for refreshing your meditation memory of Archetypes
as you move forward through each of the 12 zodiacal signs.

During your workweek, you could set your Intention with your Moon Meditation.
On the days you're not going to the office or other job or meetings,
catch up with yourself through all your Archetypes.

Set your "Intention" for the day with the Archetype of the day's Moon from the Tarot-Archetype Essences (pages 45-47). Do this particular Moon Meditation at least once through all 12 Signs. As your comfort level increases, begin understanding how to work with additional Archetypes to be included in the meditation with the Moon Archetype of the day. That will be based upon your own table of *Basic Moon Aspects for Transit Analysis* (created from the example table of Moon Transits for Female A on page 73).

Do not hesitate to ask your Guide for assistance with any step in this process.

When you finish meditating with the Moon Sign Archetype, thank him or her
with a hug, and let this Archetype go for now.

Ask your Guide if there is anything else he wants you to hear.
If not, give him a hug, thank him, say goodbye for now.

Instruct your animal to walk with you back to your cave entry,
then out of your Inner Landscape, through your cave, and into your Outer World.
Wriggle your toes, and feel your feet on the floor.

Basic Moon Meditation Template
(After meeting the Archetypes with the First Questions)

Signs/Archetypes: ♈ Aries (Emperor), ♉ Taurus (Hierophant), ♊ Gemini (Duality), ♋ Cancer (Chariot), ♌ Leo (Strength), ♍ Virgo (Hermit), ♎ Libra (Justice), ♏ Scorpio (Death), ♐ Sagittarius (Temperance), ♑ Capricorn (Old Pan), ♒ Aquarius (Star), ♓ Pisces (the Moon)

Use your Astrological Calendar to see when the Moon goes into each next Sign.

Date	☽ Moon in (Sign) (Archetype)	House in my Chart	Write notes indicating your understanding of the brief keywords for the Sign and Archetype Essence of the Moon Energies Influencing this day. Indicate your experience of meditating with that Archetype and how you were affected by day's end.

Advancing Your Daily Moon Meditations
Outline and Template

Outline: – Write Moon Sign of the day and the House being transited.

– For a sense of the Energy Influences, use *Some Keywords for Zodiac Signs and Horoscope Houses* (pages 6-12), *Quick-Reference Keywords for Planets and Luminaries* (pages 13-14), and the *Tarot – Archetype Essences* (pages 45-47).

– Write out the Moon Aspects (☽ ☌ ✶ □ △ ☍) to the planets and Sun, in your birth chart and/or to your Personal Moon (☽).

– Interpret the aspects (a good reference for a sense of the Energy Influences is *Planets in Transit* by Robert Hand).

(Before continuing with this meditation session, be sure you've previously met the specific Archetypes with your Guide and have gone through the First Questions with them, or meet them now with your Guide and do the First Questions.)

– Assuming you've met them, ask your Guide to bring the specific Archetypes involved in the aspects.

– Either work with them separately, or ask your Guide to form a circle of hands with you and all the Archetypes of the day's Energy Influences.

– Meditate with them according to the pertinent aspect notes, asking for assistance, confirmation, or make another request.

– Once you've completed your interaction, balance everyone's energies in a circle of hands – feel the energy, and let your Guide be the one to release hands before you thank them and let them go.

Template

Create and use your 12 Daily Moon Sign Archetype pages for achieving your objectives with the added energy source the Moon of the day brings.

It is recommended that you prepare separate pages for each of the 12 zodiacal signs. A folder or binder with 8½ x 11 paper is convenient for quick reference during your meditation session.

These pages will emphasize the Energy Influences of each Moon Sign Archetype. As you become comfortable writing out the keywords for the Moon aspects to the planets and Sun in your birth chart, you will likely want to include the Archetypes of those additional Energy Influences into your IGM.

Include:

- Sign description
- House number (1-12) and brief description of the House (see *Some Keywords for Zodiac Signs and Horoscope Houses, pages 6-12*).
- Aspect notes (☌ ✶ □ △ ☍) the current Moon Sign makes to the Sun ☉, Moon ☽, and/or planets in your birth chart, as shown on your table of Moon Transits.

Organize your <u>daily objectives</u> toward your <u>monthly Intention</u> for
New Moon Cycle Goal Setting and Planning (page 148).
Notice how the Moon phases work with the daily Moon moving through the Signs.

Let's go swimming . . .

If you feel as though you don't have time to do it all, you're correct!
So <u>schedule</u> everything,
and if something isn't part of the plan, let it go!
Ed to Elle

Demystifying Daily Personal Moon Times
for Setting an Intention and Timing Your Actions

(Use your birth chart and a daily Astrological Calendar for your time zone showing general Moon aspects.)

The daily Moon (☽) transits every Sign every month and makes the same aspects to the individual birth chart every month. The following exercise demonstrates how to calculate the timing of personal Moon transits for taking particular actions accordingly. Once our Daily Moon Meditation sheets are written for each Sign with its aspects, we have only to calculate the timing of our actions. Often, just the awareness of the Moon's transit to one's personal Sun or planets is sufficient. As you progress in your IGM process, this will likely be a very useful additional tool.

The idea is to set your intention with the Archetype of the day's Moon, and for a sense of the Energy Influences, use *Some Keywords for Zodiac Signs and Horoscope Houses* (pages 6-12) and *Quick-Reference Keywords for the Planets and Luminaries* (pages 13-14). See page 66 for a template of the *Daily Moon Meditation*.

Here are two sample exercises to help simplify knowing the times when the Moon is making aspects to the planets and luminaries in your birth chart.

For your daily planning,
look at the times noted on the calendar for the Moon aspects,
and look in the back part of the calendar or other ephemeris for the degrees
of the planet being aspected by the Moon on the Astrological Calendar.
Adjusted for your time zone, this gives you a sense of the timing of the Moon's transits
to <u>your</u> planets, to your own Moon, and/or to your Sun.

First Example and Exercise

The Astrological Calendar could indicate ☽ ☍ ♇ 7: 47 p.m. on a given day.
You would look at the ephemeris in the calendar for Pluto (♇ or ♇) degrees on that date,
<u>and</u> at the degrees – maybe 9° – in the sign of Capricorn (♑).

Then, look at your birth chart for the following Sign glyphs:
♑ Capricorn
♓ Pisces and Scorpio ♏
♈ Aries and Libra ♎
♉ Taurus and Virgo ♍
♋ Cancer

On a sheet of paper, write the aspect(s) to ♑
☌ ♑
✳ ♓ and ✳ ♏
□ ♈ and □ ♎
△ ♉ and △ ♍
☍ ♋
allowing the following orbs for each one:
7° +/- for ☌ □ △ ☍
5° +/- for the ✳

If the aspect is in orb, you can match it within a close time-frame to
☽ ☍ ♇ 7:47 p.m. as stated on the calendar.

This process will be easier once your table of Moon Transits is created,
and the next exercise demonstrates both how to see the timing and how to create an aspect table.

Second Example and Exercise

This sample exercise uses a Jim Maynard 2013 Astrological Calendar for the Sagittarius(♐) ☽ starting at **8:13 p.m.** (PDT), March 30, and the birth chart of Female A on page 72, and *Moon Transits for Female A* (page 73).

1. Orb used: +/–7°

2. Use the daily calendar to see the times for aspects from the Moon. Both the Astrological Calendar ephemeris and the American Ephemeris for the 21st Century 2000–2050 at Midnight can be used for the Sun and planets.

3. Both ephemerides are at GMT, so use the degrees shown for the day <u>after</u> March 31 (April 1) for the workable degrees in this exercise (when the Moon moves into a different Sign earlier in the day than this example, use the degree set in the line above that of the current day).

4. In Female A's birth chart, Sagittarius ♐ is seen in the 12th House with Neptune ♆ 6°. This is a conjunction with the transiting Sagittarius ☽ ♐ . Adding 7°, the conjunction ends at 13°.

5. Let's follow the timing of the Moon's transit to the Sun and planets up to the end of the Moon's transit through Neptune 13°.

6. The calendar shows no aspects from the Moon on March 30.

7. Looking at **March 31**, the first Moon aspect is at 3:15 a.m. square Neptune in the sky: ☽ □ ♆ .

8. Look at the ephemeris in the back of the calendar to see March 31/April 1, Neptune (♆) Pisces (♓) 4°, so we know the Moon is square to Female A's Neptune at 3:15 a.m.: ☽ □ ♆ .

9. Use the same process with the next Moon aspect at 10:41 a.m. trine Uranus ☽ △ ♅ .

10. We see Uranus (♅) Aries (♈) 8° in the ephemeris, so at 10:41 a.m. the Moon continues to be conjunct Neptune ☽ ☌ ♆ in the chart.

11. The transiting Sagittarius (♐) Moon is trine the Sun in Aries (☽ △ ☉ ♈) at 11° on April 1 for March 31, 3:14 p.m. PDT, and the Moon conjunct Neptune ☽ ☌ ♆ continues for Female A.

12. Continuing to look for when the Moon in the sky is no longer conjunct the Sagittarius Neptune (☽ ☌ ♆) in Female A's chart, we see on the Astrological Calendar that the Moon is in opposition to Jupiter (☽ ☍ ♃) at 4:03 p.m.

13. The ephemeris shows Jupiter at 11° Gemini (♃11° ♊); so, the Moon continues its conjunction with Neptune in Female A's chart.

14. At 4:44 p.m., the Moon moves into a trine with Venus in Aries (☽ △ ♀ ♈) at 12°, so the Moon conjunct Neptune is within the 7° orb.

15. At 7:13 p.m., **March 31**, the Moon square Mercury in Pisces (☽ ☐ ☿ ♓) at <u>14</u>° ends the Moon's transit over the Sagittarius Neptune in Female A's chart.

This process gets easier over time and can be very useful for planning.

FEMALE A CHART

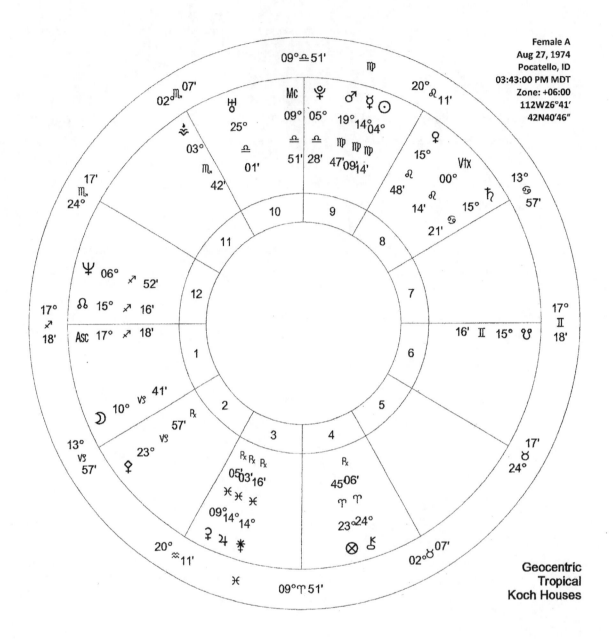

Female A
Aug 27, 1974
Pocatello, ID
03:43:00 PM MDT
Zone: +06:00
112W26°41'
42N40'46"

Geocentric
Tropical
Koch Houses

Moon Transits for Female A

(Energy Influences between Signs, Planets, and Luminaries)

This Table can be used for relationships between all Signs, planets, and luminaries; however it is being used here for only the daily Moon sign transits to Female A's birth chart. To create a template for the daily Moon sign transits to your own birth planets, luminaries, and Chiron (⚷), you could use the Signs down the side and these planetary symbols within your table.

Ascendant	Moon	Sun	Mercury	Venus	Mars	Jupiter	Saturn	Uranus	Neptune	Pluto	N. Node	S. Node	Chiron
ASC	☽	☉	☿	♀	♂	♃	♄	♅	♆	♇	☊	☋	⚷

☽ Moon Signs (1st House)	☌ Conjunction +/-7° (Compatibility +/-)	✶ Sextiles +/-5° (Opportunities)	□ Squares +/-7° (Challenges)	△ Trines +/-7° (Can be Easier/Smoother)	☍ Oppositions +/-7° (Climactic +/-)
Sign Symbols and Abbreviations					
♈ Aries (Ar)	Chiron Ar 24°/H4		Saturn Can 15°/H8 Moon Cap 10°/H2	Venus Leo 15°/H8 Neptune Sag 6°/H12 N.Node Sag 15°/H12 ASC Sag 17°	Pluto Lib 5°/H9 MC Lib 9° Uranus Lib 25°/H10
♉ Taurus (Tau)		Saturn Can 15°/H8 Jupiter Pis 14°/H3	Venus Leo 15°/H8	Sun Vir 4°/H9 Moon Cap 10°/H2	
♊ Gemini (Gem)		Venus Leo 15°/H8 Chiron Ar 24°/H4	Jupiter Pis 14°/H3 Sun Vir 4°/H9 Mercury Vir 14°/H9 Mars Vir 19°/H9	Pluto Lib 5°/H9 Uranus Lib 25°/H10 MC Lib 9°	Neptune Sag 6°/H12 N.Node Sag 15°/H12 ASC Sag 17°
♋ Cancer (Can)	Saturn Can 15°/H8	Sun Vir 4°/H9 Mercury Vir 14°/H9 Mars Vir 19°/H9	Chiron Ar 24°/H4	Jupiter Pis 14°/H3	Moon Cap 10°/H2
♌ Leo (Leo)	Venus Leo 15°/H8	Pluto Lib 5°/H9 Uranus Lib 25°/H10 MC Lib 9°		Chiron Ar 24°/H4 Neptune Sag 6°/H12 N.Node Sag 15°/H12 ASC Sag 17°	

☽ Moon Signs (1st House)	♂ Conjunction +/-5° (Compatibility +/-)	✶ Sextiles +/-5° (Opportunities)	□ Square +/-5° (Challenge)	△ Trines +/-5° (Can be Easier/Smoother)	☍ Oppositions +/-5° (Classic +/-)
♍ Virgo (Vir)	Sun Vir 4°/H9 Mercury Vir 14°/H9 Mars Vir 19°/H9	Saturn Can 15°/H6	Neptune Sag 6°/H12 N.Node Sag 15°/H12 ASC Sag 17°	Moon Cap 10°/H2	Jupiter Pis 14°/H3
♎ Libra (Lib)	Pluto Lib 5°/H9 Uranus Lib 25°/H10 MC Lib 9°	Neptune Sag 6°/H12 N.Node Sag 15°/H12 ASC Sag 17°	Saturn Can 15°/H6 Moon Cap 10°/H2		Chiron Ar 24°/H4
♏ Scorpio (Sco)		Moon Cap 10°/H2 Sun Vir 4°/H9 Mercury Vir 14°/H9 Mars Vir 19°/H9	Venus Leo 15°/H8	Jupiter Pis 14°/H3 Saturn Can 15°/H6	
♐ Sagittarius (Sag)	Neptune Sag 6°/H12 N.Node Sag 15°/H12 ASC Sag 17°	Pluto Lib 5°/H9 Uranus Lib 25°/H10 MC Lib 9°	Jupiter Pis 14°/H3 Sun Vir 4°/H9 Mercury Vir 14°/H9 Mars Vir 19°/H9	Chiron Ar 24°/H4 Venus Leo 15°/H8	
♑ Capricorn (Cap)	Moon Cap 10°/H2	Jupiter Pis 14°/H3	Chiron Ar 24°/H4 Pluto Lib 5°/H9 Uranus Lib 25°/H10	Sun Vir 4°/H9 Mercury Vir 14°/H9 Mars Vir 19°/H9	Saturn Can 15°/H6
♒ Aquarius (Aq)		Chiron Ar 24°/H4 Neptune Sag 6°/H12 N.Node Sag 15°/H12 ASC Sag 17°		Pluto Lib 5°/H9 Uranus Lib 25°/H10 MC Lib 9°	Venus Leo 15°/H8
♓ Pisces (Pis)	Jupiter Pis 14°/H3	Moon Cap 10°/H2	Neptune Sag 6°/H12 N.Node Sag 15°/H12 ASC Sag 17°	Saturn Can 15°/H6	Sun Vir 4°/H9 Mercury Vir 14°/H9 Mars Vir 19°/H9

CHAPTER TEN

TEMPLATE FOR DAILY MEDITATION

When you are not doing the Basic Moon Meditation, this is a template for meditations at the next level, after having met your Archetypes.

Sit for meditation in an upright position with eyes closed and legs and arms unfolded.

1. Enter your cave (without watching yourself).
    - Feel your feet on the ground and the air around you and notice the airflow, the smell, and how you feel.

2. Go out of the doorway to your left, and your protective animal will be waiting at that aperture.

3. Acknowledge the animal and tell it to take you to your Inner Guide (always be with the animal and your Guide on the Inner Plane).
    Follow without meandering or being distracted, and go to the location where you meet your Guide.

4. Greet him and ask whether there is anything he wants you to hear, and, if not, ask him to please let you know immediately when there is something he wants you to hear today.
    (Suggested language asking specific guidance for what you wish to accomplish today): "Please advise my thoughts, words, and actions so I . . ."
    - This is a great time to write or otherwise record your discussions with your Inner Guide.
    - Ask him to assist you in getting closer and closer to Center.
    - Talk with him about whatever is on your mind, and ask for guidance specifically from him or to be guided during this meditation session to the appropriate Archetype(s).
    - Go over the previous day's events with him, if you didn't do that before now.

5. Greet your Shadows, and thank them for their assistance the previous day. Ask them what they need from you this day, to stay at home within you and to be your full, conscious, and equal partners to keep things moving in your life. (Remember, they will never tell you to do something you cannot do and never tell you to do something that would cause harm.)
    - Ask them to
        - help you set appropriate boundaries
        - keep you from stealing energy from the possibility your life is
        - stay with you in all one-to-one interactions
        - assist you in letting people feel validated in your presence with no harm to you
        - bring helpful strangers

    - protect you from self-sabotage

    - assist you in taking a spiritually superior action or approach in a particular situation.

6. Hug them and ask them to stay with you throughout this meditation session.

7. Ask your Guide to bring your Consciousness Resistant Factors (CRFs), forming a circle of hands.
   - Greet each of them.
   - Ask what they each need from you to stay conscious and healthy at home within you and their consciousness <u>receptive</u> energy not projected out onto others. (If they don't need anything from you in this instant, ask them to let you know throughout the day if they do need something from you.)
   - Let your Guide release hands first.
   - Thank them, and ask them to stay awhile longer.

8. Now, ask your Guide to bring the Moon Archetype of the day; greet the Archetype, and use the correlating Energy Influences to help you set your intention for the day. You will find it convenient and confirming to prepare Moon Meditation sheets for each of the 12 zodiac signs, so that when you get to this point in your IGM session, you can work seamlessly with these Archetypes. The Table format on page 49 will help.

9. Ask your Guide to bring your Basic Archetypes (Board of Directors) into a separate circle of hands with him, you, your protective animal, and your Shadows. Acknowledge their power to change your life in a heartbeat and express gratitude for their wise counsel. Your Board can express its vote on the question of your personal I Ching when you do the toss in its presence. This can further inform your decision-making process.

10. Ask your Guide to bring them into the circle of hands with your CRFs.
    - Ask them to
    - bring their power and gifts to the circle so you are better able to break through to being all of yourself on the Outer Plane while staying secure on the Inner Plane.
    - work together to ensure the smooth flow of communications, decision-making, and good judgment throughout the day.

11. Thank them all, and ask your Guide to release the circle so all of you can go up to the home of your Solar Center.

12. Once there, and after being greeted by your Solar Center, ask your Guide to form a circle of hands with your Alien Energy Constructs, Inner Mother, Guide, Shadows, and all your other Archetypes (some of whom may be there ahead of you) around a deep pool of water – your *brain pool*.

13. Ask everyone to stay with you throughout the day, focusing on the good of all with no detriment to you.

14. You or your Guide may then say, "Let's go swimming" (and everyone jumps in all together to go *Swimming in Your Brain*). You may, of course, ask your Guide to close the session with just the circle of hands, in which case, let him be the one to release hands, first. Either way, that will end this meditation session. Be sure to ask your Guide to bring any of them to you during the day, as needed.

15. Come back through your cave, and walk into your Outer Plane – wriggle your toes, and feel the floor or ground under your feet.

You could set up your daily page as follows:
On the left side of the page:
Day, Month, Year
Current Moon Phase (see specifics on page 148, New Moon Phase Cycle for Planning and Goal Setting):

• Write the current New Moon Cycle phase: New Moon, Crescent Moon, First Quarter Moon, Gibbous Moon, Full Moon, Disseminating Moon, Last Quarter Moon, or Balsamic Moon

• Write the keyword(s) for the current phase: Intention; Foundation; Risk; Allow In; Fruition/ Integration; Disseminating; Take Responsibility for; or Channel/Unleash.

• Write the Tarot Archetype, Court card or Minor Arcana card drawn for the current phase and keyword(s).

• Write keywords for the Archetype, Court card, or Minor Arcana card drawn. Use the Tarot-Archetype Essences (page 45-47) or other source, such as, Mary K. Greer's *Tarot for Your Self* for Aces, Court Cards, and Minor Arcana.

To the right, in the center of the page: Write/speak with your Guide about anything on your mind – the objective is to center yourself and your intentions for the day. "Please advise my thoughts, words, and actions so I . . .." (writing your objectives for the day).

Q

Quintiles
in your birth chart?

Do daily with *Genius*!

You will not want to miss meditation
with <u>these</u> Archetypes –
they hold your *exceptional* talents!

CHAPTER ELEVEN

ENERGY INFLUENCES

Astrological Transits

The energy cycles of all life are based upon an invariable Subtle Law.
All natural phenomena are in a continuous process of change
with constancy as the underlying principle.
Heng, Hexagram #32

Transit, as defined in *Roget's International Thesaurus* (4th Edition):
passage, transference, change-over, conversion/change to something different, shift, transition

By definition, then, *astrological* transits are temporary. On the one hand, we have to take advantage of the obvious opportunities brought by favorable transits such as the connecting (aspecting) trines and sextiles and, on the other, transform the less obvious opportunities brought by transits; such as, conjunctions, squares, and oppositions. Transits provide a time-frame of *possibilities* in the moment with consequences beyond.

Given that no transit is "permanent," we understand it is our response to a transit that determines how long it affects us. For example, based on the Gregorian/Julian calendar, the Moon transits each of the 12 zodiacal signs over approximately 2.5 days a month, with a void-of-course range of a minute to more than a day before moving into the next zodiac sign. The Sun transits each zodiac sign over one calendar month, and the transits for planets through each sign range from less than a month to 14 years.

People who are unaware of transits often fall victim to the misconception that someone else's momentary attitudes or actions are simply permanent "aspects" of the individual's makeup. We have free will to change or heal what is either in our birth chart or how the celestial bodies influence us by transit. The keys are awareness and a willingness to learn how we might modify our responses to the Energy Influences of transits.

While we cannot *always* delineate specific effects of transits, we can determine reasonably accurate affects by relating the keywords of planets, luminaries, zodiac signs, and their basic aspects to our own circumstances. It is an additional method by which to navigate life and complements what is our blueprint/birth chart. We view every transit as an opportunity – we just have to know how to take advantage of each one on a timely basis.

In this book, the purposeful use of astrological transits is the awareness of the connections among the planets and luminaries to our personal charts. That awareness provides a "heads up" to the opportunities and challenges those connections show individually, collectively, and meteorologically. Naturally, some transits are more impactful than others, and, by experience, we determine which are more/less personally true. Meditating with our Archetypes for the best use of their Energy Influences for the good of all and not to our detriment assists us in knowing when to take action and how to otherwise wait for better timing.

The purpose of the I Ching is to infuse the realm of human activities with
the same clarity found in the principles of nature.
Jien, Hexagram #39

We are <u>all</u> "under the influence" – *Energy Influences*, that is.

We all learn differently . . .
Transits are valuable tools for <u>timing</u> our actions.
The earlier we learn about our true personal *gifts* – and the best timing for *showing* them –
the earlier we can consciously determine our own realistic path of contribution and fulfillment.

In fact, many of us have great difficulty learning about life in general,
and specifically about living a *virtuous* life.
What comes "*natural*" or by "*second nature*" is often harmful to us personally
and certainly harmful to the collective whole
and possibly to the Earth.

If we don't learn early from our family life, we simply must take responsibility later
for <u>finding</u> and <u>using</u> "tools" that work for us, individually, to help us learn
how to live a virtuous life, how to live with others,
contribute something meaningful in this life experience, and
derive great fulfillment from the choices we make.

Why Plan in A Vacuum?
Know the dates favored for your intention.

General transits in astrological calendars show what's going on for all of us at the same time. *Personal* transits show the current connection between what's going on with the planets and luminaries in the sky and your birth chart. Through personal transits, you will learn what action to take and when to take action for the desired result or when to lay low for your own good and/or for the good of all. High Energy Archetype relationships (squares and oppositions) will be prominent and a regular part of your meditations, so you will have the opportunity to strengthen <u>their</u> relationships and <u>your</u> relationship with them. You will get less grief from Archetypes during challenging transits and more assistance from them on the Outer Plane, because you will begin to understand the time-sensitive nature of responsibilities, promises, opportunities, feelings, beliefs, positions, points of view, and events.

<u>Plan</u> for your future –
<u>Live</u> in *now* time!
The *moment* is the only time over which you have any control.
Transits keep us "on purpose"
and <u>in the moment</u>!

Rewire your brain to live according to your transits.
Through them, you will know
when you have the greatest and least support for your objectives.
Transits activate your Archetypes, and
if you ask, they will assist you in working through
the issues and opportunities transits bring.
You will feel *rewarded*!

Moon Transits . . .
They help keep you in *now* time.

The Moon in the sky is a trigger for aspects to, and in, your birth chart planets and luminaries by

Conjunction ☌
Sextile ✶
Square □
T-Square T
Grand Cross +
Trine △
Opposition ☍
Quincunx ⚻

The Moon is the Earth's only natural satellite. It is at perigee (the point in its orbit *closest* to the center of Earth), a distance of 222,756 miles (356,410 kilometers), that we see the highest tides, the effect of the gravitational pull of the Moon. At its apogee (the point in its orbit *farthest* from the center of Earth), a distance of 254,186 miles (406,697 kilometers), we see low tides. The power of the Moon's gravitational pull affects all life on Earth.

Astrologically, the Moon is most closely associated with human emotions. If we follow the Moon's daily motion by transit to our own birth chart, we can have greater control over our reactions to its motion and, therefore, greater control of our emotions. Externally, our personal Moon represents money, cash flow, and good relations with the females in our lives, as well as the public. If our Moon's feminine energy is blocked, our money is blocked, and our relationships suffer. When we follow our Moon transits, we learn what actions bring the best results under each Moon Sign, and we learn when not to take any particular action at all. In the Inner Guide Meditation, to the extent we have a good relationship with our *Inner* Mother, our health, finances, and relationships on the Outer Plane are also good.

The motion of the Moon (13.2° a day/approximately ½° an hour) (cseligman.com) is quite discernible for some of us and not for others. Many people may find it significantly more useful to track the moon on a daily basis according to zodiacal signs in calendar form, such as the Jim Maynard series of calendars and according to the New Moon cycle phases for planning and goal setting (see page 148). Moon tracking resources such as these can be used in conjunction with following when the Moon is void of course and when we are in a personal void of course Moon.

Void of Course Moon

(Partially adapted from information provided by Michael Munkasey and Signe Quinn Taff, Astrologers)

This astrological condition of the Moon has been recognized for more than 2000 years and acts as a balancing mechanism for human emotional and intellectual conditions.

The "Void of Course Moon" (V/C ☽) is a period of time released by the Moon as it moves through the sky and refers to the period of time the Moon is "in between" Signs. The General V/C ☽ occurs at the same time for everyone (though according to the respective time zones; e.g., if the general V/C Moon occurs at 9:00 a.m. on the west coast, it is occurring at the same moment but at 12:00 p.m. on the east coast).

An example of the moon being in between Signs is when the Moon leaves the sign of Sagittarius and hasn't yet moved into the next sign of Capricorn. The length of time for a V/C ☽ can be a minute or more than 24 hours. It is definitely a time during which we chill, take a "time out." If you need to commute anywhere when a General V/C ☽ is continuing from the night before into commute hours, it is recommended that you allow double time to reach your destination by a certain time, as traffic conditions are more likely to impede your commute plans.

General Void of Course Moon (V/C) and the Personal Void of Course Moon (PV/C)

There are general Void of Course Moon periods, and our Personal Void of Course Moon (PV/C ☽) dates and times, which coincide with or precede the general V/C Moon. The distinction is important to know and use in conjunction with the general V/C Moon dates and times. When we are not in our personal void of course Moon, we still have to work within the parameters of the general V/C Moon – it just won't be quite as frustrating as the unwanted and unintended consequences of actions taken in the PV/C or plans that fall through, when made during one's personal void of course moon. Remember, however, most people have no clue whether they are in a PV/C, so we use the rules of a general V/C just to keep things copacetic (if that's even possible).

The PV/C ☽ is a signal we are vulnerable to circumstances beyond our control. If we know the dates and times of our PV/C ☽, we figure out what we can and cannot do during the PV/C ☽. For example, it would not be the time to take (elective) tests, do an interview, or have any important meetings, present ideas in meetings, start a new job, have surgery (unless it is an emergency, of course), and certainly not start a partnership or business, or get engaged – let alone married. It is best to plan nothing, decide nothing in particular, commit to nothing, and purchase nothing major. If we do, we should expect the result to be very different than we intended. Other examples of actions taken in a V/C ☽ include failed businesses, countless accidents, jobs taken that don't last, romances that go nowhere, marriages or other partnerships that ultimately fail, as well as major and minor purchases that are major disappointments and repairs that require RE-repair.

On the national stage, examples of unintended consequences due to actions planned or taken during a V/C ☽ include President Nixon's nomination for President and also his election in 1972; the Watergate break-in; and President Ford's swearing-in ceremony. The 2000 Presidential Election is another example: Al Gore's nomination in a V/C ☽ for, and acceptance of, the nomination to be the Democratic party standard-bearer for President <u>and</u> Joe Lieberman's nomination for Vice President; as well as the 2000 Election Night results, various court proceedings related to the 2000 Election, and results.

In the 2008 Presidential Election, Barack Obama was nominated by Hillary Clinton to be the 2008 Democratic party standard-bearer for President during a V/C ☽, and Joe Biden accepted his nomination to be the Democratic party Vice President during a V/C ☽. On Election Day, November 4th, the Moon was Void of Course until 4:01 p.m. Finally, the *official* time for a new President is 12 Noon EST on January 20th. At that time, in 2009, the Moon was Void of Course; therefore, Barack Obama became President during a V/C ☽.

In terms of its legal significance, Barack Obama was first sworn in at 12:10 p.m. (V/C ☽ and in Mercury Retrograde, when communications are often more challenging), and Chief Justice John Roberts misspoke – placing "faithfully" at the end of the sentence rather than correctly before the word "execute"). On January 21st, 2009, at 7:35 p.m. (not in a V/C ☽) then-President Obama retook the Oath from Justice Roberts. Arguably, the lack of support from the Moon (extrapolated to Congressional support) at the original swearing-in caused the bulk of President Obama's agenda to be stopped or otherwise made it much more difficult for him to garner minimal support for fulfillment of various change issues in his first term. President Obama's swearing in for his second term, on January 20, 2013, at approximately 11:50 a.m. EST, was in a Taurus Moon; thus, not in a V/C ☽, nor was he in a PV/C ☽.

Plan Ahead . . .
Know your Personal Void of Course Moon dates and times.
Use an Astrological Calendar to stay aware of specific <u>general</u> Moon transits.

Essential Dignities
(Using Rulership and Exaltation in Transits)

In addition to identifying the aspects to and from the Moon and Sun (luminaries), consider whether the Moon or Sun is in Rulership as it transits a given Sign. Look also at whether the Sign on the House cusp rules the House being transited. The Rulership gives additional power or strength to the planet or Sign or House.

While you may be identifying aspects only between the Moon and Sun now, the Rulerships and Exaltations are shown here to familiarize you with them for later use. The Rulership or Exaltation of the luminaries and planets in the Sign or House transited exerts the most powerful Energy Influences on them. Accidental Rulership indicates the House "ruled" by the planet or luminary shown on this list.

Sign Rulership of Planets/Luminaries		House of (Accidental) Rulership
Sun Leo	☉ ♌	5
Moon Cancer	☽ ♋	4
Mercury Gemini	☿ ♊	3
Mercury Virgo	☿ ♍	6
Venus Taurus	♀ ♉	2
Venus Libra	♀ ♎	7
Mars Aries	♂ ♈	1
Mars Scorpio	♂ ♏	8
Jupiter Sagittarius	♃ ♐	9
Jupiter Pisces	♃ ♓	12
Saturn Aquarius	♄ ♒	11
Saturn Capricorn	♄ ♑	10
Uranus Aquarius	♅ ♒	11
Neptune Pisces	♆ ♓	12
Pluto Scorpio	♇ ♏	8

Sign Exaltation of Planets/Luminaries		House of (Accidental) Exaltation
Sun Aries	☉ ♈	1
Moon Taurus	☽ ♉	2
Mercury Aquarius	☿ ♒	11
Venus Pisces	♀ ♓	12
Mars Capricorn	♂ ♑	10
Jupiter Cancer	♃ ♋	4
Saturn Libra	♄ ♎	7
Uranus Scorpio	♅ ♏	8
Neptune Cancer	♆ ♋	4
Pluto Leo	♇ ♌	5

Find out about and take advantage of <u>your</u> best timing –
during the day, the month, <u>and</u> each year!
Start as soon as possible –
ASAP!

Just like a savings account, the "energy" accumulates interest now
and builds for the future.

Let's go swimming . . .

CHAPTER TWELVE

TRANSITS ACTIVATE OUR ARCHETYPES

Once we begin <u>using</u> personal transits, our Archetypes are acknowledged
and take an active part in our lives at our request.
You will <u>want</u> their assistance. Ask!
They bring healing revelations, renewal, and serenity.

Whatever House Saturn (♄) in the sky is transiting in one's birth chart,
the Energy Influences of <u>our</u> personal Saturn are also carried to that House.
We meditate with our Saturn (World) Archetype and the Archetype of the Sign through which
and where Saturn in the sky is transiting in our own birth chart.

Example
Saturn may be in the Sign of Capricorn (♑) in the 10th House of your birth chart.
Saturn in the sky may be transiting your 8th House in the Sign of Scorpio (♏).
Saturn in the sky is making a 60° ✶ (sextile) aspect to your own Saturn.

The Archetypes representing these Signs and Saturn are
World (♄ /Saturn)
Old Pan (♑ /Capricorn)
Death (♏ /Scorpio)

You would look in the *Tarot – Archetype Essences* (page 45-47) for their basic Energy Influences
and at the *Some Keywords for Zodiac Signs and Horoscope Houses* (pages 6-12).

You would write the pertinent phrases from those two lists
for World/ ♄ , Old Pan/ ♑ , and Death/ ♏
and for the House in your birth chart through which Saturn is transiting.

You would then ask your Guide to bring these Archetypes before you,
and when they are present, you would let them know you're aware
they can show you opportunities for self-mastery toward your social destiny.
Ask them to work together to show you where are you limiting yourself,
and ask how to enhance powers of transformation.
Ask what they need <u>you</u> to do that will speed up the process.

You would then ask your Guide to join everyone in a circle of hands to check their unity.
Feel into the energy of the circle.
Let your Guide release hands first; then, thank everyone, and let them go.

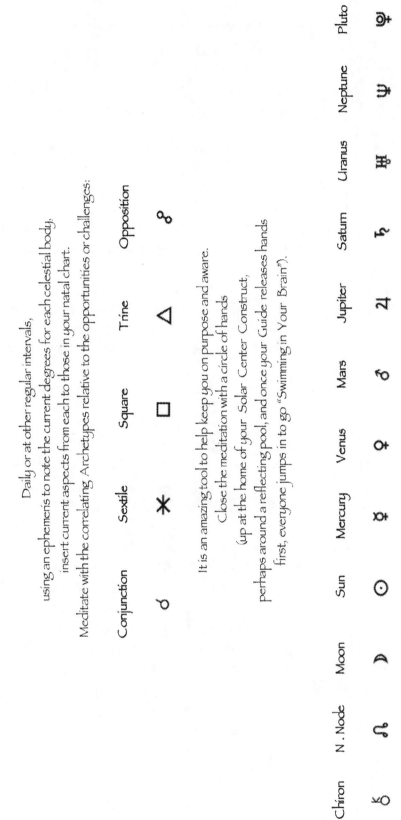

Template for Transit Meditation with All Your IGM Archetypes

Daily or at other regular intervals,
using an ephemeris to note the current degrees for each celestial body,
insert current aspects from each to those in your natal chart.
Meditate with the correlating Archetypes relative to the opportunities or challenges:

Conjunction	Sextile	Square	Trine	Opposition
☌	✳	□	△	☍

It is an amazing tool to help keep you on purpose and aware.
Close the meditation with a circle of hands
(up at the home of your Solar Center Construct,
perhaps around a reflecting pool, and once your Guide releases hands
first, everyone jumps in to go "Swimming in Your Brain").

Sun	Mercury	Venus	Mars	Jupiter	Saturn	Uranus	Neptune	Pluto
☉	☿	♀	♂	♃	♄	♅	♆	♇

Moon	N . Node							
☽	☊							

Chiron								
⚷								

Transits bring adventure . . .

We can't *"dally"* with them,
and we also don't need to *"cave"* <u>under</u> them!

Transits are gifts,
whether they bring a "heads up"
about a challenge <u>or</u> an opportunity.

Make no mistake,
the transits bring "power" for us to *borrow* for a finite amount of time.
Learn to <u>use</u> your current transits,
and move to the next level of consciousness through your Archetypes.

So, what if you have a very difficult birth chart, fraught with limitations?
Chances are <u>great</u> that if you learn to work with and operate within transits,
you'll be able to accomplish something worthwhile for the good of all
in spite of the difficulties in your personal blueprint.

Let's go swimming . . .

Planning with Your Archetypes

Aside from calculating your overall transits on a regular basis, so you don't miss a warning or an opportunity,
plan ahead for the following transits with your Archetypes, and, unless otherwise noted,
allow a few days before and after the exact date to take advantage of their Energy Influences:

☉ ☌ Asc

Sun conjunct Ascendant
A new start of a personal nature.

☉ ☌ ☽

Sun conjunct Moon
The best time all year to make changes of a personal nature.

☉ △ ♂

Sun trine Mars
Things start moving in your direction.

☉ □ ♂

Sun square Mars
Leave no loose ends.

♂ ☌ ♂

Mars conjunct Mars
This is the best time for favorable results to your actions.
Start a new project; ask for a salary increase; apply for and start a great job.
Allow a month on both sides of the conjunction.
The farther away from the conjunction, the farther from having the ♂ ☌ ♂ support.

♂ ☍ ♂

Mars opposition Mars
This is definitely *not* the time to count on a salary increase or find/start a great job.
Take an interim position.
Expect several months to a year on both sides of the opposition.

♀ △ ♀

Venus trine Venus
The best time to attract beneficial relationships, cooperation,
and circumstances, as well as engage in highly creative endeavors.

Meditate with the Archetypes of the Sun, Moon, planets and their Signs,
asking for specific results and for the best possible outcomes.

When We Work within Personal Transits
we are working in harmony with the Universe as it relates to our own birth chart,
and <u>timing</u> our actions is more in line with our personal nature.

So, we <u>are</u> collectively all "one," <u>and</u> we're individuals within that oneness.

Key #1
Awareness

Key #2
Using the opportunity or heeding the challenge
by working with your Archetypes.

Find out the dates key transits can work for you
and those transits which can create obstacles to your efforts.
Mark your Astrological Calendar
with <u>*your*</u> transits, not just the <u>general</u> transits.

Key #3
Meditate with those Archetypes
to prepare yourself for their best and highest use
for manifestation on the Outer Plane.

The Grand Cross

We all experience a Grand Cross three times a month through Moon sign transits
and four times each year through Sun sign transits!
Our energy gets scattered in four directions.

Prepare ahead with the Archetypes in the Grand Cross to balance
interpersonal flexibility, effectiveness, and relaxation.

To focus otherwise scattered energy during the transit, meditate with
the Archetypes of the planets, Sun, and/or Moon Signs
which are △ and/or ✳ to the Grand Cross planets, Sun, and/or Moon.

Being <u>un</u>aware, we can get *stuck* under the Energy Influences
of these four 90° angles (two 180° ♊ opposing axis)
when the Moon transits each Sign for <u>part</u> of the 2 ½ to 3 days Moon transit, and
when the Sun transits each one of the four Signs throughout the year.
We have to look for ways to productively balance and centralize the energy of all four
Signs/planets/luminaries.

Write the House cusp degrees of your birth chart and
for each Sign, the planets, and/or Sun and Moon inside the Houses.

You will notice that opposite Sign/House cusps have the same degrees.
When the Moon and/or Sun are within +/– 7° of all four House cusp or celestial bodies,
they are creating a Grand Cross.
Aside from illness (forced relaxation),
examples of how the scattered energy creates *stuck-ness* include the following:

The Cardinal Grand Cross

Aries (♈), Cancer (♋), Libra (♎), Capricorn (♑)
The easiest Grand Cross to handle.
We exert too much energy without focus and without a complementary amount of relaxation.

The Fixed Grand Cross

Taurus (♉), Leo (♌), Scorpio (♏), Aquarius (♒)
High inner tension due to frustrated needs and blocked intentions,
creating vulnerability to explosive reactions and sometimes destructive actions.

The Mutable Grand Cross

Gemini (♊), Virgo (♍), Sagittarius (♐), Pisces (♓)
We may allow others to make decisions for us or are otherwise too easily influenced by outside influences.
There's a need to define ourselves and our own truth and take greater self-responsibility.

Oh, by the way . . .
We <u>also</u> get a Grand Trine with each Moon Sign!

We can plan ahead for these three times each month using this formula:
Write the degrees for each of the following House cusp Signs
and planets, plus the Sun and Moon inside each House.
When the Moon and/or Sun are within +/– 7° of <u>all three</u> Signs and/or celestial bodies,
a Grand Trine condition is created.

Examples of how you might use these Energy Influences include the following:

Fire Grand Trine
(♈) Aries, (♌) Leo, (♐) Sagittarius
Initiate actions based on confidence.

Earth Grand Trine
(♉) Taurus, (♍) Virgo, (♑) Capricorn
Use practical determination and methodical precision for calculated ambition.

Air Grand Trine
(♊) Gemini, (♎) Libra, (♒) Aquarius
Take advantage of opportunities to influence others for the good of all
with sheer intellect and idealism.

Water Grand Trine
(♋) Cancer, (♏) Scorpio, (♓) Pisces
Nurture others with intuition, wisdom, and sensitivity.

Transit Triggers
Mark your Astrological Calendar for *transit triggers*.

Example
Say, for example, you have a T-square in your birth chart
(two opposing celestial bodies both square a third at 90° angles)
3° ♂ ♈ (Mars Aries)   11° ♃ ♎ (Jupiter Libra)
10° ♅ ♋ (Uranus Cancer)

the T-square would be activated each month at Moon (☽) 4° in any of
the three Signs (allowing −7° orb from the highest 11°).
It is <u>de</u>activated at ☽ 10° of any of the three
(allowing +7° from the lowest 3°).
Meditate with Tower, Emperor, Fool, Chariot, Wheel of Fortune, and Justice,
asking them to assist you in making the most creative use of this T-square.

Be sure to calculate the orbs accordingly . . .
Sextiles ⚹ +/-5°
Squares ◻ +/-7°
T-Squares T +/-7°
Grand Crosses + +/-7°
Trines △ +/-7°
and
Oppositions ☍ +/-7°

Use a calendar showing daily Moon Signs
as well as an ephemeris
(which may be in the back of your calendar)
to track aspects from the planets/luminaries to your birth chart.
Knowing the transit dates ahead of time is
a heads-up for you to prepare with
specific Archetypes to advantageously *shift* Energy Influences.

You'll find it useful to get in the habit of tracking these before they begin.
Don't take in any energy you cannot afford.
Meditating with your transit Archetypes assists in shifting energies
away from a negative experience to just AFGO.

CHAPTER THIRTEEN

TRANSIT TALK

Every transit has to play out, so we work with our Archetypes to shift
Energy Influences as necessary, to something <u>less</u> traumatic and <u>more</u> supportive.

Use these tools:
Keywords for Zodiac Signs and Horoscope Houses (pages 6-12)
Quick-Reference Keywords for Planets and Luminaries (pages 13-14)
Tarot-Archetype Essences (page 45-47)

With squares and oppositions between "friends"
(i.e., trines △ and sextiles ✷),
the challenge is easier, and
the opposition ☊ is less difficult or negative.

Example
Uranus trine Pluto (♅ △ ♇) in a birth chart carries its higher energy
to any <u>transit</u> of Uranus to/from Pluto.

Key
Meditate with Fool (♅) and the Archetype of zodiac sign it is <u>transiting</u>, and
add Judgment (♇) and the Archetype of its Sign <u>from the birth chart</u> to
align with these positively life-altering Energy Influences.

Conversely, if you already have "issues" through squares and oppositions
in your birth chart, a transit can make it worse, especially if you ignore the transit.
You have to bring the Archetypes together, and
let them know you need them to shift the harm and injury they *could* cause
to something radically transformative of a <u>positive</u> nature.
(See When you Work on Problems, page 113.)

Be as specific as possible within their areas of responsibility.

Example
Looking at Saturn (♄) in Scorpio (♏) square (□) to 9th House Pluto (♇) in Leo (♌),
we know Pluto rules Scorpio, and Scorpio forms a natural square to Leo,
<u>and</u> Pluto is <u>exalted</u> in Leo,
so the challenge Saturn in Scorpio brings to Pluto in Leo is somewhat diminished.

Key
Meditate with World (♄), Death (♏), Judgment (♇), and Strength (♌)
to minimize challenges other people may cause for you in 9th House matters.

We have to get down to the basics of our own transformation,
make important changes – let go of one thing to gain another –
to better organize our lives and re-define ourselves.

Mandala for Planets Moving through Your Birth Chart

1
Use a saucer-sized plate to draw a mandala circle.

2
Divide the mandala into 12 pie slices, numbered 1-12.

3
From your birth chart, note the Signs on the cusps of each House,
and draw the corresponding glyphs on each House of the mandala.

4
Use an ephemeris
(e.g., in the back of a Jim Maynard Astrological Calendar)
to see the Signs being transited by the planets and the Sun.

Draw the glyphs for the planets and Sun
in the corresponding House of those Signs in the mandala.

5
Insert the dates of the transits on the outside of each House.

6
Make notes of what transpires during those transits related to each House.

CHAPTER FOURTEEN

MERCURY RETROGRADE (☿ ℞) TRANSITS

Awareness of some particulars about Mercury Retrograde goes a long way!

Mercury (☿) is the smallest of the planets with its diameter being half that of the Earth. It rules Gemini (Ⅱ) and Virgo (♍) and represents one's ability to communicate with others without impediment, as well as one's thought processes – as in faster. (See *The Arcana Dictionary of Astrology* by Fred Gettings.) All the planets have retrograde cycles, as do the Nodes and Chiron. The Sun and Moon, as luminaries, do not have retrograde cycles.

In retrograde, from an astronomical perspective, Mercury appears to be going backwards against the backdrop of fixed stars – like a vehicle on the freeway passing a train going the opposite direction. Astrologically and physiologically, it can interfere with communications at every level – as in slower. (See *Karmic Astrology – Retrogrades & Reincarnation* by Martin Schulman and *Retrograde Planets* by Erin Sullivan.)

Many of you know the drill: we have to <u>count on</u> greater misunderstandings, as all communications are likely to suffer. We have to expect delays, undelivered mail, and messages. Expect to write and rewrite in the present and wish to rewrite the past. Always get repairs done of any kind before Mercury Retrograde begins, or wait until it ends.

Emergencies excepted, Mercury Retrograde is definitely *not* the time to start a new relationship, a new job, or long-term project; it is not the time to enter into binding commitments (marriage, financial, or otherwise) without the absolute expectation of necessary modifications, alternative compromises and/or reversals in the original plan and/or intent. Unless it's an emergency, it is generally not a good idea to make or go to medical appointments during Mercury Retrograde.

Interpersonally, communications at all levels are likely to be problematic, and we are inclined to <u>think slower – process communications slower</u>! <u>Use</u> Mercury Retrograde for deeper thinking about any subject, issue, or idea. We have to be patient with each other <u>and</u> ourselves.

Expect computer issues – not the least of which will likely include slower connections (also, we MUST back up data).

Expect misleading information.

Expect missed appointments, traffic problems, the failure to keep one's word because of a promise that could not be kept, misplaced documents, more computer-related problems.

Any Mercury Retrograde cycle is *the* time to <u>re</u>-think, <u>re</u>-do, <u>re</u>-define, <u>re</u>-organize, <u>re</u>-assess, <u>re</u>-orient, and/or <u>re</u>-plan without taking action on the "new plan" until after Mercury Retrograde ends. It is the time for completions; i.e., cleaning up paperwork, paying old debts, doing what we've promised that hasn't been completed or otherwise handling those matters responsibly.

It is not the time for repairs to machinery or automobiles in particular; chances are, repairs have to be made to the repair! It IS the time to chill – to spend time *thinking* more than expanding our activities; <u>planning</u> what to change and how to move forward after Mercury Retrograde ends. Think of it as an *opportunity* that comes around three or occasionally four times a year for three to four weeks.

No one escapes the discomfort of Mercury Retrograde – wherever we have Gemini (♊) or Virgo (♍) in our birth charts, we are going to experience the effects of any Mercury Retrograde cycle. However, "awareness" is sometimes the key to being *less* affected.

Mercury "rules" those individuals with a Gemini or Virgo Sun. Those with a Gemini Sun, Moon, or Ascendant will, most likely, be in the uncomfortable position of having to re-think precisely where they are most comfortable; i.e., in easy, adaptable communications suitable for the moment. On the other hand, for the Gemini who is aware of Mercury Retrograde, the opportunity exists to clarify communications – being so precise there is little room for misunderstanding.

Virgo Sun (♍☉), Moon (☽), or Virgo Ascendant (Asc) will likely experience the usual difficulties presented by a Mercury Retrograde cycle; however, their main opportunity is to analyze how they may be the carping critic and unnecessarily complicating matters for themselves and everyone with whom they are in contact by vague communications. Another issue could be analyzing everything to death with slower reasoning powers, so all the analyzing actually gets in their way. Other issues may be intolerance for disorder or totally rationalizing a double standard they might be using to manipulate a situation.

During Mercury Retrograde, we are all being forced to loosen our grip on immediate plans and expectations in order to relax, reconsider plans, re-think positions we have taken, and refresh ourselves until the cycle ends. The first half of Mercury Retrograde is the time for the greatest reflection and introspection.

During the second half of Mercury Retrograde, people will be especially inclined to just get on with business/life as usual – they start getting impatient. There is likely to be tension stemming from a new perspective and the added awareness that we are literally blocked from doing what we feel ready to do to the fullest extent. Where we *should* focus is physical, mental, spiritual, and emotional well-being, as well as plans for greater fulfillment in our lives *after* the cycle ends.

Sleep deprivation during Mercury Retrograde can cause extreme confusion, inflexibility, and general difficulty staying in reality-based thought. When we feel the least bit sleepy, it is extremely important, not to mention refreshing, to just STOP what we are doing and close our eyes for a few minutes.

Mercury Retrograde affects all modes of travel and all modes of communication. It is definitely not a favorable time for travel, and we should do so *only* when our personal Energy Influences show positive indications. (See Informing Your Decision about Traveling in Mercury Retrograde page 103.) Expect greater stress in any event. Also, it is no secret that when people text and drive, the distraction can cause disastrous accidents. During Mercury Retrograde, the hazard is multiplied when those who are so busy texting they go through red lights or don't stop for pedestrians on a busy street, or even see animals (and animals can't think).

Whether we are pedestrians or behind the wheel of a vehicle – it will pay dividends to take an extra ten seconds for a second and a third look before leaving a STOP sign or a GREEN signal light to go!

Informing Your Decision about
Traveling in Mercury Retrograde (☿ ℞)

The easiest way to find out whether the ☿ ℞ transit affects your individual birth chart during Mercury Retrograde is the following:

1. Look in an ephemeris for the date during Mercury Retrograde you wish to travel.

2. Write the degree of ☿ Mercury for that date. Allow for the Greenwich Mean Time (GMT) time difference (if the ephemeris you're using is based on GMT) – which usually means to look at the degree for the _next_ day.

3. Look at your birth chart for your own Mercury to see whether it is in a Sign that is ☐ (90°/square) or ☍ (180°/opposite) the Sign of the current Mercury Retrograde.

4. Do the same process for ♂ Mars and the ☉ Sun.

5. And don't forget to check dates and times for your Personal V/C Moon _and_ the General V/C Moon.

6. Also look at _Personal Transits to Inform One's Travel Decisions_ during Mercury Retrograde. (See page 104.)

7. Do your personal I Ching toss process (pages 134-137) with your Board of Directors (Basic Archetypes) present, to inform and balance your thinking. Once you've made a decision, confirm it with your Guide.

Personal Transits to Inform Your Travel Decisions During Mercury Retrograde

Barring any emergency, when deciding whether to travel during Mercury Retrograde, the following transits to our personal planets add to the stress and delays, as well as communication and computer issues:

☿ ℞ □ ☿ **Mercury Retrograde square our own Mercury**: Among the vulnerabilities of this transit, expect a lack of mutual understanding, obstacles in short trips, lateness for appointments or commitments, long waits for a scheduled appointment even if we arrive on time, misplacing documents.

☿ ℞ ☍ ☿ **Mercury Retrograde opposing our own Mercury**: Communications are especially difficult – especially when it comes to saying what we're thinking or intending. Communicate, travel, and make decisions only as necessary.

☿ ℞ □ ☉ **Mercury Retrograde square our Sun**: Don't expect cooperation, let alone credit for your actions. Expect to defer to someone else's plans. People tend to be disagreeable, rude, crude, and annoying.

☿ ℞ ☍ ☉ **Mercury Retrograde opposing our Sun**: Don't rely on others to keep their word, and there is considerable difficulty agreeing about what needs to be done and how to get it done. Conflict and ill-will are prevalent.

☿ ℞ ☍ ♂ **Mercury Retrograde opposing our Mars**: Vulnerability to verbal abuse; arguing for the sake of causing problems; fault finding; critical lack of attention to detail; communication interference; more accidents on our route; and being more easily distracted. There is a tendency to take impulsive action, causing unplanned negative consequences. It's more difficult to keep track of our own luggage and/or arrive somewhere on a timely basis when someone else is in control of the transportation.

♂ □ ☊ **Mars square our North Node**: This is an extremely unfavorable transit for group activities, where vulnerability to someone else's impulse can bring misfortune to us.

♂ ☍ ☿ **Mars opposing our Mercury**: This is an extremely unfavorable transit for air travel, as it is likely there will be greater turbulence and more traumatic events; communications tend to be highly charged; and vehicle breakdowns are more prevalent – not to mention we may have far too much work to be completed to even contemplate traveling for enjoyment.

♂ □ ☿ **Mars square our Mercury**: People are more impatient, critical, and ready get into a confrontation with anyone who doesn't say what they want to hear. News is upsetting and/or disturbing. There's a greater possibility of flights being cancelled after check-in. Ground traffic is more problematic than usual.

♂ ☍ ☉ **Mars opposing our Sun**: There are longer delays, our own energy is depleted, and unpleasant encounters with people who have strong attitudes are exhausting. Ticket agents are likely to cause us grief.

♂ ☌ ♅ **Mars conjunct our Uranus**: Extremely unfavorable for travel; we are more vulnerable to fire danger; highly vulnerable to being involved in an accident; sudden drastic actions are often necessary; erratic and irrational travelers; explosive impatience and outbursts; sudden hostility.

♂ ☍ ♅ **Mars opposing our Uranus**: This is another extremely unfavorable travel indication, fraught with danger from sudden, shocking, unexpected events, conditions, and/or blunt or violent encounters that can subject us to extreme tension and strain and requiring maximum self-control. There is a greater possibility of electrical outages and mechanical failures. One can only hope a flight is cancelled.

☉ □ Asc **Sun square our Ascendant/Rising Sign**: People are more inclined to be working against our best interests – most likely unintentional, but Mercury Retrograde can bring out the worst in people.

CHAPTER FIFTEEN

FOUR DIFFICULT BIRTH RETROGRADE (℞) TRANSITS
Early awareness is an important start.
Meditation with the appropriate Archetype is key.

1. **Mercury Retrograde (☿ ℞)** is a much maligned and feared cycle – let alone fearing its visit upon new born children. <u>Many</u> people are born when Mercury is in retrograde. The effect depends on the Sign and House in which Mercury is posited, as well as aspects to and from Mercury. It would be useful to have a professional Astrologer interpret the Mercury Retrograde found in one's natal chart. The younger one is shown/taught to recognize the various possible adverse effects of ☿ ℞, the earlier its issues can be properly addressed through the IGM. By age 7, a child may begin learning to meditate.

From a general astrological perspective, thought processing/priority is different between those whose Mercury was in retrograde motion at birth and those whose Mercury was in direct motion at birth.

From a human perspective, the unique way of looking at things through the ☿ ℞ lens can be used to appropriately contribute to the good of all and achieve success in a meaningful position in society where one born with ☿ ℞ skills can thrive. It's not always easy for others to understand what the ☿ ℞ individual is trying to communicate. The *essence* of his/her knowledge often gets blocked by over-emphasizing a basic idea, not being able to correctly process communications in the moment, and responding too fast with the wrong words or an angry outburst. Life <u>is</u> harder. The individual born in ☿ ℞ will always need to strive for intellectual independence at the same time she or he also strives to be understood.

More than other children (or even more than many adults),
You may not "get" the importance of brushing your teeth at least two times a day
– let alone flossing –
until after you've had many cavities, root canals, and crowns.

Your actions may be inappropriate for what's actually going on around you –
even the way you pose (or don't) for a group photograph.

You may learn differently than current teaching methods being used.
You may want or need to think more deeply about something than time permits;
e.g., you may need three hours for a thirty-minute school exam.
You may need to study longer and harder than other people, so
it might be a fine line between "extra" activities with friends and getting homework done.

You may be disruptive in the classroom.
You may frustrate your teachers and other students.
You may be bullied, or you may <u>be</u> the bully.
<u>You</u> may feel frustrated and not *understand* or even *recognize* the difficulty.

Dance on your limitations.

Learn to meditate with your Magician (☿ ℞) Archetype and the *Sign* in which the Magician lives.
The Magician can get in the way and slow your progress unless acknowledged and
consciously included in your thought processes about intentions.
Learn to speak carefully from <u>intention</u>, and
make certain your Magician and you are working *together.*

Align your rational mind with the creative process,
to communicate original ideas through your ☿ ℞ Magician.
Learn about your inner strength and courage from your Tower Archetype.
In moments of anger, seek a spiritually superior response through your Magician <u>first</u>.

Find out about and <u>honor</u> the needs of your ☿ ℞ Magician Archetype and
the Archetype of the *Sign* in which it is placed.
Understand what they both need, because that will open the door
to greater *self*-exploration of what <u>you</u> need
in order to operate together in your best interest in the moment and beyond.

Similar to the *general* Mercury Retrograde transit,
your commitments generally may have to be modified,
unless you give *extra* thought to what the commitment means,
and have your calendar with you to make plans.

Allow *extra* time to mentally process contracts and their fine print.
Be fully prepared to honor all commitments, and to otherwise be responsible about changing them.

Be humble – be aware!
Know that you <u>do</u> think differently than many others.
Strive to understand <u>how</u> you're different
from those who do not live with Mercury Retrograde day in and day out.
Honoring your ☿ ℞ Magician, you are more introspective,
more retrospective, and possibly more skeptical.

Stake your reputation on your integrity,
and don't apologize for what <u>others</u> don't understand about you.

During Mercury Retrograde (☿ ℞) transits,
<u>your</u> ☿ ℞ doesn't "go away."
You may notice that *others* experience the worst of ☿ ℞,
because they may not have learned
how to use it as an opportunity to re-evaluate ideas, goals, and positions.
You have to be extra cautious because *everyone* <u>then</u> experiences what <u>you</u> experience daily.

Don't dwell on the *issues* your ☿ ℞ Magician may cause you.
<u>Do</u> work diligently with the Magician to *use* that energy to deepen your brain pool.

Let's go swimming . . .

Parents can learn more about their child's birth chart with exact birth data given to a Professional Astrologer.

If the retrograde glyph ℞ is on ☿ (Mercury), read and learn about many of the possible effects of Mercury retrograde in humans and understand possible impediments,
as well as encourage the strengths of that particular retrograde during childhood and adolescence.

Three Other Difficult Birth Retrogrades
Early recognition and regular meditation with
the Archetypes of retrograde planets in one's chart are imperative.

Keeping in mind that the Sign and House of the retrograde planet are key,
as well as its aspects to the luminaries or other planets in the birth chart,
here are a few difficulties often experienced by those born with these planets in retrograde:

♂ ℞
Mars Retrograde
Tower Archetype Difficulties:
Coordinating thoughts with actions; regulating energy flow
Goal setting and follow-through
Regulating one's drive for self-expression and self-definition
Seething inside without an appropriate release mechanism

♄ ℞
Saturn Retrograde
World Archetype Difficulties:
Vulnerabilities to environmental energies
Weak or absent father figure; unstable sense of authority
Slow maturation process
Rigid, self-defeating habits/rules
Indiscriminate socializing/fluctuating social boundaries

♆ ℞
Neptune Retrograde
Hanged Man Archetype Difficulties:
Not trusting one's intuition
Not easily understood by others
Deluded, chasing unrealistic fantasies
Trying to make the present dream fit with reality
Finding a spiritual path for Inner security

(For deeper study, see *Additional Reading Opportunities* or Schulman and Sullivan books on Retrogrades.)

CHAPTER SIXTEEN

SWIMMING DEEPER

Barometers
Measures of Change
Everyone to whom we are related, by blood, law, or role,
acts as a barometer for specific areas of our lives.
(See pages 246-252 of the IGM book for a description of how to insert these individuals into your birth chart.)

We are all connected by the two-way energy flow of *projection*. Ed created this barometer so anyone with high skepticism would have hard evidence – fact – (not fiction, no fantasies) that the meditation works. How these people react and handle the events in *their* lives from our perspective serves to show how *we* are handling events in the area of our chart where they vibrate.

People who vibrate to these areas will change as we
meditate with our Archetypes to heal these areas of our lives.
This, of course, assumes we *want* to change how we operate in these areas.
If so, it is not that we understand the barometers in new ways; <u>they</u> often start doing <u>new</u> things!
The information that they are, in fact, doing new things comes to us either directly or through others.
However, if what *we* must do to effect that result is to compromise *ourselves*,
we have to accept responsibility for the consequences.

Family Barometer Meditations
Track outer planet transits
– Uranus (♅), Neptune (♆), and Pluto (♇) –
on your Family Barometer chart to see whether you need to meditate
to shift unfavorable energy to more positive, productive, and constructive use.

Example
Someone in the family (by birth or law) has a heart attack, but it is not fatal.
The energy of that individual is in the House where you have Pluto (♇).
Uranus (♅) is transiting the Sign on your Pluto.
This suggests that you need to make some kind of judgment
and radical change in that House.

In meditation, you would ask your Guide to bring your Judgment (♇) Archetype, and ask:
"What kinds of changes do I need to make that I haven't been making?"
"What potential is untapped, unrecognized, or is not integrated within me?"
"What destructive instinctual drive needs illumination in me?"

Once the changes are being made, the "heart attack" energy will likely be diminished.

The Inner Guide Meditation Barometer Chart

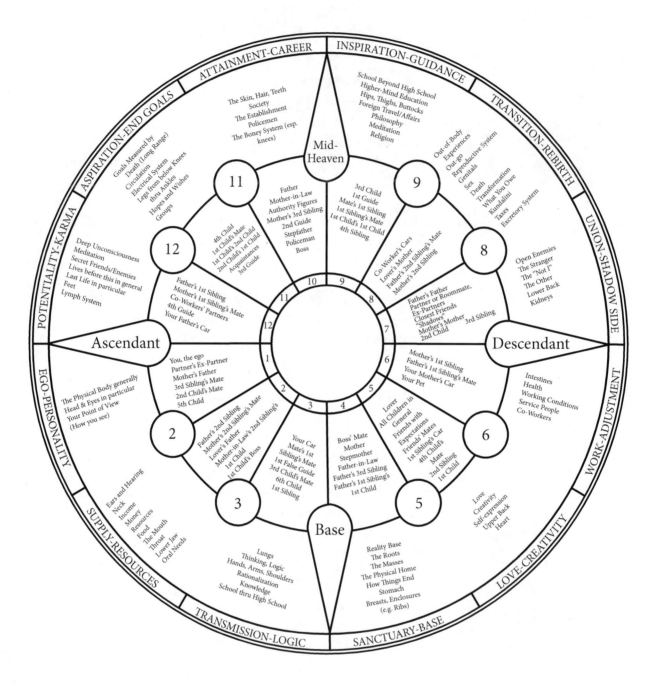

When You Work on Problems
Focus on <u>solutions</u> – not on the problems; focus on <u>answers</u> – not questions.
Denis Waitley (**est** Workshop Leader)

(These instructions assume you've already met these Archetypes;
if not, you will want to do that prior to using this process.)

1. Look for the apparent problem in one of the Houses on the Barometer chart (page 112). For example, the issue might be your job (not to be confused with career). "Job" and working conditions are 6th House matters. (Other things are associated with the 6th House, but for purposes of this example, "job" is useful.)

   - On a separate piece of paper, write the House number in which the problem can be found (in this case, 6th).

2. Using example Female B Chart (page 114), note the Sign on the 6th House cusp is Virgo (♍), with both Mars (♂) and Venus (♀) in the 6th House in Libra (♎). Write both Virgo (♍) and Libra (♎).

3. Female B's Archetypes (page 115) or Tarot-Archetype Essences (pages 45-47) show Hermit as the Archetype for Virgo and Justice as the Archetype for Libra. Also write the Archetypes "Tower" for Mars (♂) and "Empress" for Venus (♀).

4. Always meditate with the Archetypes in the House where the problem is located, except we aren't using Archetypes for asteroids Ceres (⚳), Pallas (⚴), Vesta (⚶), and Juno (⚵), which you may also see in your own birth chart.

5. Explain the problem to the Archetypes, and ask them what they perceive to be the problem or the reason for the problem. Ask what each needs from the other to remedy the situation. (You are asking the Archetypes related to the problem what they need from each other to ease – if not resolve – the problem.)

6. Ask each one to say what she or he needs in return from the other in order to help resolve the problem. The Quick-Reference Keywords for Planets and Luminaries (pages 13-14) may be helpful in understanding the possibilities suggested by these Archetypes.

7. Ask whether they will agree to do what the other requests. (If not, give them permission to say why, and work with them toward a compromise.) If there's an impasse, explain to them that when they don't cooperate, or when they act as separate energies within you, they cause major upsets in your daily reality that impede your progress. Ask your Guide to intercede.

8. Once they agree, ask what they all need from you to work cooperatively to make this happen. (It will be something totally doable and never harmful.)

9. Assure them that you will do it, and have everyone hold hands in a circle with you and your Guide. Let your Guide be the one to release hands first before you thank them all and say goodbye for now.

FEMALE B CHART

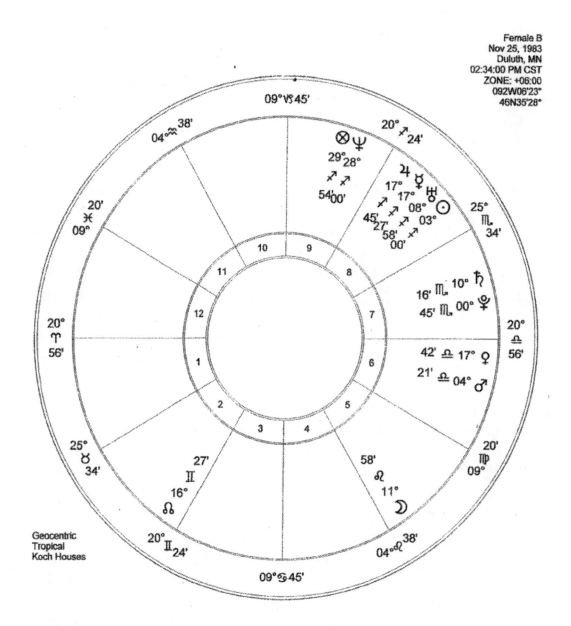

Female B's Archetypes

	House & Sign	Archetype for Sign	Ruler/Planet/Nodes	Archetype for Ruler/Planet
1	♈ Aries	Emperor	♂ Mars	Tower
2	♉ Taurus	Hierophant	♀ Venus	Empress
	♊ Gemini	Duality/Lovers	☿ Mercury	Magician
			⚷ Chiron/N.Node ☊	Chiron/N.Node
3	♊ Gemini	Duality/Lovers	☿ Mercury	Magician
4	♋ Cancer	Chariot	☽ Moon	High Priestess
5	♌ Leo	Strength	☉ Sun/Moon**	Sun/ High Priestess
6	♍ Virgo	Hermit	☿ Mercury	Magician
	♎ Libra	Justice	♀ Venus/Mars ♂	Empress/Tower
7	♎ Libra	Justice	♀ Venus/Mars ♂	Empress/Tower
	♏ Scorpio	Death	♇ Pluto/Saturn ♄	Judgment/World
8	♏ Scorpio	Death	♇ Pluto/Saturn ♄	Judgment/World
	♐ Sagittarius	Temperance	♃ Jupiter/Sun ☉	Wheel of Fortune/Temperance
			♅ Uranus/Mercury ☿	Fool/Magician
			☋ S. Node	S. Node
9	♐ Sagittarius	Temperance	♃ Jupiter/Neptune ♆	Wheel of Fortune/Hanged Man
			⊗ Joy*	
10	♑ Capricorn	Old Pan/Devil	♄ Saturn	World
11	♒ Aquarius	Star	♅ Uranus/Saturn ♄	Fool and World
12	♓ Pisces	Moon***	♆ Neptune	Hanged Man

* Arabic Part of Fortune

** Personal Moon

***Not the Personal Moon

CHAPTER SEVENTEEN

BUILDING RELATIONSHIPS

Projection
If you're going to "project" anything,
project on the <u>Outer</u> Plane how you feel about *yourself* on the <u>Inner</u> Plane.
(Ed, in discussion)

Also,
when we push our own creative energies away from
the awareness of our egos,
we will draw to ourselves creative people who will live out those energies for us.
(IGM, page 19)

While we never work with images of known people from the Outer World
when we are working with energy forms in our Inner World,
a useful exercise on Projections is one Ed suggests
about asking our Guide in meditation to bring Outer World figures to take their
true energy form as they live in our Inner World
and seeing the images we *project* on them.
(IGM, page 115)

Heads Up!

Nod your head yes, and
keep choosing what you chose,
by keeping your word.
est Aphorisms

Handle your agreements responsibly . . .
You may not <u>keep</u> your agreement,
but handle that responsibly
(with an acknowledgment and, where possible,
offer or request an alternative).
Adapted from **est** Aphorisms

Zodiac Sign Relationships to Build Upon
in Meditation and Person-to-Person

Meditate with the Archetype of the planet or luminary transiting the Signs indicated
on one or more of the following lists:

Zodiac Sign Relationships to Build Upon and Not to Be Taken for Granted or Abused
or
Planet/Luminary Transit Opportunities Not to Be Missed, Wasted, or Abused
or
Zodiac Sign Challenges and Rewards If Handled Well in Meditation or Person-to-Person

Zodiac Sign Relationships to Build Upon
and Not to Be Taken for Granted or Abused

For you:	Build upon these relationships with your Archetypes:
♈ Aries	♌ Leo and Sagittarius ♐
♉ Taurus	♑ Capricorn and Virgo ♍
♊ Gemini	♒ Aquarius and Libra ♎
♋ Cancer	♓ Pisces and Scorpio ♏
♌ Leo	♈ Aries and Sagittarius ♐
♍ Virgo	♑ Capricorn and Taurus ♉
♎ Libra	♒ Aquarius and Gemini ♊
♏ Scorpio	♓ Pisces and Cancer ♋
♐ Sagittarius	♈ Aries and Leo ♌
♑ Capricorn	♉ Taurus and Virgo ♍
♒ Aquarius	♊ Gemini and Libra ♎
♓ Pisces	♋ Cancer and Scorpio ♏

Planet/Luminary Transit Opportunities
Not to Be Missed, Wasted, or Abused

For you:	Opportunity is found by transits through these Signs:
♈ Aries	Aquarius ♒
♉ Taurus	Pisces ♓
♊ Gemini	Aries ♈
♋ Cancer	Taurus ♉
♌ Leo	Gemini ♊
♍ Virgo	Cancer ♋
♎ Libra	Leo ♌
♏ Scorpio	Virgo ♍
♐ Sagittarius	Libra ♎
♑ Capricorn	Scorpio ♏
♒ Aquarius	Sagittarius ♐
♓ Pisces	Capricorn ♑

Zodiac Sign Challenges and Rewards
If Handled Well in Meditation and Person-to-Person

For you:	With planets or luminaries transiting these Signs:
♈ Aries	♋ Cancer and Capricorn ♑
♉ Taurus	♒ Aquarius and Leo ♌
♊ Gemini	♓ Pisces and Virgo ♍
♋ Cancer	♈ Aries and Libra ♎
♌ Leo	♉ Taurus and Scorpio ♏
♍ Virgo	♊ Gemini and Sagittarius ♐
♎ Libra	♋ Cancer and Capricorn ♑
♏ Scorpio	♒ Aquarius and Leo ♌
♐ Sagittarius	♓ Pisces and Virgo ♍
♑ Capricorn	♈ Aries and Libra ♎
♒ Aquarius	♉ Taurus and Scorpio ♏
♓ Pisces	♊ Gemini and Sagittarius ♐

However people communicate with you,
it's the highest they can do, at this time.
est Communication Workshop

Respect and Relationships

The whole meaning of life is continual self-cultivation –
taking the opportunity to positively reform oneself on a daily basis.
Lu, Hexagram #10, Line 5

Because many people don't understand when their actions are being influenced by adverse transits versus authentically from "Center," they often get "off purpose." Misunderstandings occur, and people lose respect for each other. Aside from automatic respect for one another until we personally experience something with another individual, we can increase our respect for others just by understanding that they may <u>unknowingly</u> be reacting to general transits. If we learn to operate <u>knowing</u> our *personal* transits, we can counteract being at the effect of adverse general transits, including the Void of Course Moon. Our Shadows are available to help us by merely asking, and we can meditate with the appropriate Archetypes to ensure we take a spiritually superior approach to our interactions.

In personal relationships – i.e., friends, family, lovers, mates – our Archetypes and Shadows hold the keys to successful personal relationships. Regular meditation with your Archetypes brings you to a Centered state of being. Meditate with Archetypes for the 2nd House of values, 3rd House of communication, 5th House of romance, your 7th House of one-to-one interaction and partnership, 8th House of shared emotional and material resources, your 10th House of social destiny, and your 11th House of manifestation. "Success" is measured according to <u>intention</u>, as well as the ability to hold promises as sacred, the willingness to honor commitments, self-respect, respect for each other, not taking each other for granted, and a "no"/"never" position being shifted to at least "maybe," with an honest effort to get to "yes!"

In the workplace, how do we find <u>something</u> to respect in co-workers and supervisors that makes it easy (okay, easier) to work with them? Do we need to take individual responsibility for finding something to respect in order to work well with someone we may not respect? It is often ignorance of communication difficulties in one's own birth chart that causes vulnerabilities in the workplace. Conversely, many people who work well with others have no clue about their birth charts. Is it a matter of <u>self</u>-respect that enables them to avoid relationship difficulties with co-workers?

Let's go swimming . . .

What *causes* respect?

Is it automatically just "there" or is not?

Is it based on an assumption that someone has great intelligence, wisdom, a gift or talent before being tested?

Is it based on a skill set, money, clothes, or maybe opinions that match our own?

Is it about age? Social status? Reputation? Peer pressure? Religious affiliation? Contribution to important causes?

What causes DISrespect?

Bad manners?

Is it a fear factor, a competition factor – a threat?

Is it the realization that someone is not as smart as we thought or <u>does</u> something different and not the way we wish it had been done?

Is it about age? Reputation? Peer pressure? Race? Politics? Religious affiliation? Career choice? Showing zero concern for life beyond human life?

On what *should* respect be based?

Good manners?

Popularity?

Friends?

Career choice?

Honesty? Decency?

A good work ethic?

Trustworthiness?

Good stewardship of planet Earth?

Showing respect for <u>all</u> living creatures?

Finding and Creating Respect:

In the workplace, how do we *find* something to respect in someone that makes it *easy* to work with her or him?

Do we need to take individual responsibility for finding *something* to respect, in order to work well with someone we really may *not* respect?

Is it a matter of <u>self</u>-respect that causes some people to work well with others?

What part does this fact play: We're all <u>one</u> under the Sun on planet Earth?

We are <u>all</u> "somebody" . . .

We are "all one" <u>and</u> we are all different.

It's about <u>knowing</u> who *we* are and taking a spiritually superior approach in what we <u>do</u>.

Knowing who *we* are can bring greater respect from and to us.

Don't make people "bad" and "wrong" for what *they're* saying or not saying.
What will cause a breakthrough for <u>you</u>?
Meditate with your Archetypes to shift the energy as needed
according to the circumstances and
without being self-righteous.

"I" Hexagram #27
The mouth is the opening where things
both enter and leave the body,
and it must be guarded well.

Migrate from habitual ways of interacting
to ways that are in alignment with the path of virtue,
tranquility, wisdom, and mutuality.
est Aphorisms

We can pray for all things and people *outside* of us, over which we have <u>no</u> control,
and <u>meditate</u> to take responsibility for all things *inside* us, over which we <u>need</u> to have control.

Bad-Mouthing Other People

Hexagram #8
Beh
Fellowship
Commentary
(*I Ching* page 264)
Judge yourself well and others moderately.
Do not have intimate dealings with unvirtuous people whose
words mean little and whose actions are indecisive.
Do not nourish an unfaithful person.
Do not speak of another's shortcomings at any time.

Granted, we are not going to be liked by everyone,
and it's *so* hard to learn how to
handle what <u>we</u> don't like about someone else,
let alone not repeating it to others.
But why allow that energy to take up space in our heads?

Many people don't <u>want to</u> change their own bad behavior, and
many others carry heavy "baggage" from their past.
Chances are they don't need others to make it heavier,
and we certainly don't need to add to our own.

Remember . . .
Don't allow in any energy <u>you</u> can't afford,
and toxic talk can ruin your life as well as someone else's!
(*Good luck with <u>this</u> lesson!*)

CHAPTER EIGHTEEN

HEALING AND COMPLETING UNEASY RELATIONSHIPS

People are trapped by emotions,
desires, fears, attachments
and other "enemies"
which the mind
creates.
Kun, Hexagram #47

Negativity hurled in our direction *(projections)* from others
may have as much to do with our own resistance to change
as with someone's negative feelings <u>about</u> us.

12-Step Process to Shift Negative Energy
(Use IGM, pages 113-115 Question #28)

In brief, the 12 steps involve
asking your Guide during meditation
to take you to the true energy form of that individual within you
(having no resemblance to the individual on the Outer Plane).
The form represents what you are projecting onto the individual on the Outer Plane,
which may be causing the negativity <u>toward</u> you.

As *you* change the script, the other individual will either change or leave your reality.
Ed

Make it a priority . . .

Use your transits to see and work through relationship issues.
Add it to your Template for Goal Objectives and Progress Dates (page 149).

Let's go swimming. . .

Understanding and Completion
of Upsetting Relationship Encounters

(Using the Assistance of Your Board of Directors and the *I Ching*)

1. Have your I Ching book, paper, pen, and coins at hand. You'll be doing a toss in the presence of your Board of Directors. Use pages 134-136 to guide you through the I Ching toss.

2. Go into your cave and to your Inner Landscape where your animal will be waiting, as always. Greet him or her, and ask to be taken where you where you and your Guide always meet.

3. Ask your Guide to bring any Archetype(s) on your Board of Directors who you haven't met, and then meet and do the First Questions with each Archetype (be sure to write the particulars, and get each name); thank each Archetype, and ask them to stay.

4. Then, take whatever time is necessary to look at the Table for Remembering Your Archetypes (page 49) to refresh your memory, as needed, for the rest of your Board Archetypes.

5. Ask your Guide to bring them together at the location you and he choose for Board meetings.

6. Greet them all, and introduce any new Board members by name to the rest of the Board.

7. Let them know you're seeking to better understand and be okay about the encounter(s) with (name), and you want to get their point of view about it through I Ching.

8. Write the date and time, and you could write the question as follows:
    "Invariable, kind Virtue of the Universe, please respond to the variable question of my human life. What Hexagram best describes how I can understand and process my recent encounter with (name)?"

9. Write the salient points of the Hexagram(s), and if you need further information, ask your Guide for the wording of an additional question.

10. When you have the basic information you need, thank them all, and let them go for now.

11. Add the information about any new Board members involved, to your *Table for Remembering Your Archetypes*.

12. Thank your Guide, give him a hug, and ask your animal to take you back to the entrance to your cave.

13. Go through the cave and into your Outer Plane.

14. Wriggle your toes, and feel the floor/ground under your feet.

For attempting to change the energy regarding people who are always negative toward you,
remember to use the exercise Ed suggests in response to Question #28,
Pages 113-115
in *The Inner Guide Meditation*.

Incompletions and Completions
(Adapted from **est** Workshops)

In a separate section of your workbook or otherwise on separate paper, list the following applicable "*Incompletions*" (the Sign indicated is for the corresponding House in your birth chart, and the Tarot Major Arcana names are the meditation Archetypes to speak with for "*Completion*"):

♈ Aries: Emperor/Tower

> I <u>want</u> to do and am not doing . . .
>
> I have wanted to do and <u>haven't</u> done . . .
>
> I want to complete and am not completing . . .
>
> I need to assert myself in this situation and am not . . .

♉ Taurus: Hierophant or High Priest/Empress

> I want and don't have . . .
>
> I have <u>wanted</u> to have and don't have . . .
>
> I have wanted to accumulate . . . and <u>haven't</u>.

♊ Gemini: Duality or Twins/Magician

> I want to say that I'm <u>afraid</u> to say . . .
>
> I want to say, and I am embarrassed to say . . .
>
> I want to say I don't know <u>how</u> to say . . .
>
> I have wanted to say that I don't <u>want</u> to say . . .
>
> I want and am not seeking opportunities to . . .
>
> I want and am not <u>creating</u> the opportunity to . . .

♋ Cancer: Chariot/High Priestess

> I am protecting . . .
>
> I am holding on to . . .
>
> I want to express my feelings about . . . and am afraid to.
>
> I want to express my feelings about . . . and have not.

♌ Leo: Strength/Sun

> I want to <u>prove</u> and I haven't proven . . .
>
> I haven't been acknowledged for being . . .
>
> I have done and haven't been acknowledged for doing . . .
>
> I <u>have</u> . . . and I haven't been acknowledged for having.

♍ Virgo: Hermit/Magician

> I need solitude for . . . and am not taking the time.
>
> I am complicating my life by . . . and don't know how to stop.
>
> I am vague about . . . and want to share clarity.
>
> I am using a double standard to justify . . . and I want to stop.

♎ Libra: Justice/Empress

I have to decide about . . . and can't.

I want balance between . . . and . . . but can't do what's necessary to find that balance.

I need to resolve a personal issue . . . and I justify not finding a place to start.

I want to unplug the invalidation machine and get started to solve my . . . problem.

♏ Scorpio: Death/Judgment

I give my all to . . . and I am not getting the results I seek.

I am passionate about . . . and am not pursuing.

I am not transparent about . . . and want to be straightforward.

♐ Sagittarius: Temperance/Wheel of Fortune

I've started and am not working on . . .

I <u>want</u> to start and am not yet starting . . .

I am working on and have not completed . . .

I want to experience and have not experienced . . .

I want to take a stand for . . . and have not.

♑ Capricorn: Old Pan/World

I am dissatisfied with . . .

I want to change and am not changing . . .

I <u>want</u> to be . . . and am not.

I have <u>wanted</u> to be, and I am not . . .

I fear . . . and am not acknowledging the reason . . .

♒ Aquarius: Star/Fool

I am inspired by . . . and am not . . .

I want to change . . . and am not seeking ways for creative change.

I want to change . . . and do not know where to start.

♓ Pisces: Moon/Hanged Man

I want to stop and am continuing . . .

I have sympathy for and am not helping.

I feel insecure about . . . and am not facing what's real for me.

I feel insecure about . . . and do not understand why.

I may be deluding myself and am not facing reality about . . .

Write a few of these Incompletions at a time on your Sign Goals/Goal Houses template (page 149), and meditate with your Guide and the Archetype of the applicable Sign toward completion.

When you meet your goals about the <u>Incompletions</u>, list your <u>Completions</u>.

Confirmation of Completions

What if . . .

every day there were confirming signals from the Universe
that you're on purpose?
You're acting from intention and following through with what it takes
for *completion* of your intentions.

Can you promise yourself an <u>action</u> every day
that opens the possibility of receiving that confirmation?
What action are you willing to take
as an expression of the commitment to your written goals?
(See Goals template on page 149).

Your Archetypes are just waiting for you to jump in,
and stay on purpose.
<u>Use</u> them through your transits.

There will be confirming signs you're on the right track toward your goals.

CHAPTER NINETEEN

TOOLS TO DEEPEN YOUR BRAIN POOL

I Ching
Teaches the principle of balance –
operating from this principle and
maintaining balance in all situations involving change.

The I Ching was formulated in China approximately 6,000 years ago, each line being based upon a fundamental principle of natural law. The use of I Ching is multi-faceted. When seeking the correct *I Ching Book of Changes* for your personal use, the particular edition will be evident as you immediately understand and relate to what you are reading when you open the book to any hexagram. It is important that you personally relate to the edition you select, conceivably for lifetime use.

Doing the toss for your personal I Ching questions in the presence of your Basic Archetypes (Board of Directors) is additionally powerful. Do not enter the process with a "preference." The Instruction and Result do not "ensure" that what you ask will happen as it reads; however, it increases the possibility at the moment of the toss and, additionally, informs decisions you are trying to make. It does not circumvent *free will* in the Instruction and Result given.

It is a good practice to write the exact time of the question for purposes of doing a Horary in addition to the toss, if there are complications which are unanswered in the Commentary, or if more information is needed to help in making a decision.

When you've completed the toss and have written the information given in the hexagrams, ask your Guide to affirm your understanding of them and, if additional information is needed to make your final decision, ask your Guide why the information in the hexagram might (or might not) be correct.

For quick access to this timeless tool for informing decisions and/or asking any question, when you are away from your home or office, carry a small travel kit including three Chinese coins (or pennies) and photocopies of the table of hexagrams and matching brief keywords of the 64 hexagrams (such as given in the *Book of Changes and the Unchanging Truth* by Taoist Master Ni, Hua Ching).

Questions you'll ask may be prefaced as follows and include a date or time-frame within the question:
Invariable kind virtue of the Universe, please respond to the variable question of my human life. What is the result for the good of all if _____, by (date or within a set period of time)?

Examples of various types of inquiries include:
- Show me the hexagram that will most effectively recommend what actions will heal my cold-condition.
- Show me the consequences of making this purchase at this time.
- What hexagram best directs my actions with respect to. . . at this time (or by a certain date).
- Show me how I am doing with ____ situation at this time.
- Speak to me about where I am in my progress toward achieving _____.

Specific guidelines for the toss are found in Ed's book, *The Inner Guide Meditation* (page 253), and are adapted here as follows:

- Use three coins, each with one side being heads and the other tails (preferably Chinese coins).
- Set one coin aside.
- Shake the other two coins in your hands, and gently toss them on an even surface.
- If one comes up *heads*, and the other comes up *tails*, use the *tails* coin to toss with the other coin; if both come up *heads*, use one of those coins with the one you set aside. Leave the coin in place that you did not select from the first toss.
- Use the same procedure to toss one of the original coins with the coin you had previously set aside, and count 2 for each tails and 3 for each heads.

<u>From the bottom up</u>, you would draw lines similar to these: ____ and __ __
The straight line would be numbered 7 ____, and the broken line __ __ numbered 8, unless your toss adds up to 6 or 9. Then, you would draw a broken line in the left column, and number it 6 __ __, but *change it* to a straight line ____ in the right-hand column; or, in the case of a 9 toss, you would draw a straight line in the left-hand column with number 9 ____, but *change it* to a broken line in the right-hand column __ __.

The entire procedure is repeated six times (two sets of 3 tosses each), and culminates in patterns similar to these:

7____
8__ __
7____
7____
8__ __
7____

A "fated" toss (all 7s and/or 8s) means the *Instruction* and the *Result* are combined in the same hexagram without reading changed lines or commentary.

The toss, including changed lines (from tosses which add up to either 6 or 9), gives an *Instruction* and a *Result* if you follow the Instruction. The changed lines of the hexagram for the *Instruction* are read from the 6 or 9 toss. The paragraphs of the *Result* are read up to the "Lines" section in your I Ching book, without reading that section.

X9____   __ __
8__ __   ____
7____   ____
7____   ____
X6__ __   ____
7____   ____

You then look on the Guide (Table in your I Ching book) to find the Hexagram number for the matching lines of the trigrams <u>from the top of the table down</u> (<u>with the trigrams shown</u> on the top and on the side), and from the left side of the table across to the intersecting number with the correct trigram at the top; and write the number underneath, for example:

7____
8__ __ this top set of 3 lines (trigram) represents "Li"
7____
7____
8__ __ this bottom set of 3 lines (trigram) also represents "Li"
7____
Li
30

You would then look up Hexagram #30, check the hexagram lines you just tossed to make sure they match the lines in #30, and, since it is a Fated Toss, read only the paragraphs <u>up to</u> the section indicating Lines 1 through Line 6. The Instruction and Result are contained in the paragraphs before the Lines Section.

For a hexagram containing changing lines (as shown below for Hexagrams 30 and 34), you would read the paragraphs and the changed lines of Hexagram 30 for the *Instruction*; then read only the paragraphs up to the Lines section of Hexagram 34 for the *Result* if you follow the Instruction. The *Result* may also offer additional information that confirms the Instruction.

Note that the first column below (the *Instruction*) appears to have the same lines as the above "Fated" example, Hexagram 30; however, you will note that lines 2 and 6 (from the bottom up) are changed in the second column (the *Result*):

X9____   __ __
8__ __   __ __ this top trigram represents "*Chen*"
7____   ____
7____   ____
X6__ __   ____ this bottom trigram represents "*Chyan*"
7____   ____
Li   Ta Chuang
30   34

Again, you would read Hexagram #30 first, including the changed lines 2 and 6, for the *Instruction*, and read Hexagram #34, up to and not including the "lines," for the *Result* if you follow the *Instruction*.

Remember that the I Ching *informs* your decision; it does not make the decision for you.
Also, the possibility of the event transpiring, as the hexagram reads, is *increased* – not guaranteed.
Store your Book of Changes on a shelf at a height above your shoulders.

Other Useful Questions for the *I Ching* Toss

(The I Ching book used in *Swimming in Your* Brain, suggests the kinds of questions to be considered; it is *The Book of Changes and the Unchanging Truth*, by Taoist Master Ni, Hua Ching. Almost any question may be asked; however, take your lead from your preferred I Ching reference, and be sure your question doesn't require a "yes" or "no" Instruction.)

Examples

Invariable kind Virtue of the Universe, please respond to the variable question of my human life. What Hexagram best reflects the opportunities I can look forward to over the next six months?

Invariable kind Virtue of the Universe, please respond to the variable question of my human life. What Hexagram shows the issues I may face over the next month?

Invariable kind Virtue of the Universe, please respond to the variable question of my human life. What Hexagram will assist me in resolving _____ (issue) within __ (number of days or weeks)?

Invariable kind Virtue of the Universe, please respond to the variable question of my human life. Which Hexagram best instructs how I should respond to _____ (name) at this time with respect to _____?

Additional Decision-Making Processes with Your Inner Guide, I Ching, and Tarot

Example of a Process to Use in Making a Life-Altering Decision

Say you want to consult your Archetypes about the possibility of moving in with a roommate by a date certain. You're thinking this relates to "housing" – yes, and it turns out to be a bigger question. It is best completed in two meditation sittings, a day or so apart – and, if you haven't already met all the Archetypes on your Board of Directors, it may take another day (and never in a V/C Moon).

First Meditation

(Sheets to have at your fingertips and the process to use in making your decision): IGM Barometer (page 112) – Look on the Barometer for "Contracts" and "Roommates" – you'll see it's the 7th House. You can see additional information about the 7th House in *Some Keywords for Zodiac Signs and Horoscope Houses* (page 6-12).

Table for Remembering your Archetypes (page 49) –
Look on the Table for the 7th House Archetypes.

(If you haven't met them, take a quick look at your **Tarot-Archetype Essences** sheet for an idea of their Energy, and ask your Guide to bring them before you, separately. Ask the "First Questions," and add them to your Table.)

Tell them what you're considering, give them the pros and cons as you perceive them, and ask for their perspective. Ask what they want you to further consider. Confirm with your Guide that he agrees with you and with them about what to consider *in toto*.

Second Meditation

Once you've fully considered the matter and are certain there's no deception and nothing you haven't been told by your friend (inadvertent or otherwise), ask your Guide to bring your **Basic Archetypes** (Board of Directors) to you.

(Be sure you have met each of them, or do so now.) Once you've completed that process, memorize where you will be meeting them and write out their seating chart. Include your Guide and your Shadows in the seating and in Board Meetings. Your Guide will always sit at the head of the circle, with you to his left, and your Shadows to your left. Then, complete the circle with your Board Members.

Tell them what you want to do, and take an initial vote – and your vote also counts. Your Guide doesn't vote, nor do your Shadows, but they definitely give you their opinion IF you ask (and <u>do</u> ask). Really take <u>in</u> what everybody tells you, and where there is disagreement between Board Members, ask what it will take to get them to compromise. Take a second vote, if necessary.

Do an I Ching toss to further inform your decision: "What is the result for the good of all if I . . .?" Another question might be: "*What hexagram best informs me as to the near-term result of . . .?*" Or, ask "*What hexagram best informs me as to the long-term result of . . .?*"

Finally, if your decision is in the affirmative, check your transits to be sure there's plenty of positive Energy to support the goal/intention; i.e., on the actual move date. For example, from the New Moon (a waxing Moon) is favorable until just before the Full Moon (a waning Moon). The move would likely be easier in a waxing Moon instead of a Waning Moon. Also, you don't want to sign a contract or move in during Mercury Retrograde or during a Void of Course Moon.

When Your Intuition Tells You There's *More* to Consider before Automatically Accepting an Invitation

1. In the presence of your Board of Directors with your Inner Guide and protective animal on the Inner Plane, do an I Ching toss (pages 134–137). (Remember to date and time your first "burning thought," and include a date or time period for the action or event in the I Ching question, and try not to enter into the question with a preference of Instruction and Result.)
2. When you want to additionally inform your decision, do a Horary based on the exact time of your burning question, as noted above, with the date.
3. Also, draw Tarot cards from the Major Arcana for the following questions:
    - What does it look like if I do . . .?
    - What does it look like if I do not . . .?
4. To affirm and/or to ask "why?" in order to make your final decision, speak with your Inner Guide.

Example

You may have an innocent question about an invitation for a fun "opportunity" but your intuition prompts you to do a "quick" I Ching toss.

Specifics

On one such occasion, I not only entered the question with a decided preference but wanted a quick answer to what turned out to be a deeper issue. My I Ching question was:

What is the result for the good of all if I go (to this particular event)?

Instruction #33 *Tun*: Retreat, because positive energy is retreating and negative energy is advancing. If one truly understands the situation, there is protection in retreat.
Result: #25 *Wu Wan*: Innocence/Unexpected Happening – purity of innocence from experience and knowledge; having the capacity to do something but choosing to remain innocent, and abstain because you understand the situation.

Not satisfied with the Instruction and Result, I asked the following questions in a Tarot draw:
"What does it look like if I go?" Tarot #18/Moon – emergence of the repressed, and
"What does it look like if I do not?" Tarot #19/Sun – a turn in the journey to self.

When I asked my Inner Guide *why* I should not go, he pointed out the precise issue, relating to an invasion of my spiritual space.

The Learning

The child-of-wonder innocence was based on "excitement" and fascination. The *innocence*, based on "knowledge and experience," was taught by all three processes. That is not to say there is no longer a place for *this* child of wonder to experience innocence based on excitement and fascination; it just wasn't appropriate for this event.

If not immediately, over time you will be impressed with the I Ching hexagram language
of the Instruction and Result as they specifically address your question and concerns. In this case,
the process influencing my decision not to attend the event took about 30 minutes.

Numerology
This is an extremely powerful tool barely touched on here.
It deserves your further exploration.

For example:
Change your name –
Change the effect you have on others –
Change your life!
~Plus or Minus~
Be careful!
Make a conscious choice!
Before you change *your* name, let alone name a baby,
find out what Energy Influences come with the choices.
Do an *I Ching* toss (pages 134-137) asking the result for the good of all if this name is chosen.

Formula:

```
1  2  3  4  5  6  7  8  9
A  B  C  D  E  F  G  H  I
J  K  L  M  N  O  P  Q  R
S  T  U  V  W  X  Y  Z
```

Print a name; match each letter with a number 1-9; total the numbers.
Reduce double numbers (<u>except</u> 11 and 22) to a single number.

These brief keywords are extremely simplified for purposes of "names" only.

1	Leader, courageous, highly individual
2	Sensitive, receptive, and often unreliable
3	Creative, social, harmonious, and often without cooperation from others
4	Can achieve great things and is also a magnet for negativity
5	Adventurous and often has more difficulty than most in getting along with others
6	Home and family oriented; friendships are also specifically important
7	Intelligent, spiritual; gets what he or she deserves – plus or minus/fair and square
8	Money and materiality are focal points
9	In harmony with the Universe
11	Master of creativity/inspiration
22	Master of accomplishment

Very good resources:
The Numerology Kit book by Carol Adrienne; and *Numerology* by Barbara J. Bishop

Real hope
can be based on the aspects to and from Jupiter in our birth charts
and working with the Archetypes of the Houses, Signs, planets and luminaries
through which Jupiter is <u>transiting</u> in our birth charts.

How happy do you want to be?

What do you want to *contribute* to the rest of us in this life experience?

How much of your time is spent <u>*vegging out*</u>
instead of <u>*maxing out*</u> your *Inner* resources?

Is that a luxury you can afford?
Really?

Whose dream are <u>you</u> following?
Think about it –
Can you afford to waste <u>your</u> Inner gifts just watching others use <u>theirs?</u>

Don't take a pass on *any* true opportunity to learn.
Continuing education may mean the difference between <u>being</u> a robot and <u>owning</u> one!

Kicking a Habit
Make it one of your goals.

Meditate with the Archetype of the habit,
or, if the planet/luminary is part of your Solar Center Construct,
meditate with him to help make the craving fall away.
Include the Archetype(s) in or on the cusp of the applicable House.

Examples

The Archetypes who can help kick a drug addiction are Moon (Pisces), Hanged Man (Neptune),
and planets found in the 12th House, or the Sign
on the cusp of the 12th House, if there are no planets in the House.

The Archetypes who can help kick a tobacco addiction are
Tower (Mars), Hanged Man (Neptune), and
Archetypes of planets or luminaries in the 12th House and/or the Sign on the 12th House cusp.

The Archetypes who can help kick a sugar addiction are Empress (Venus), Hanged Man (Neptune), and
Archetypes for planets or luminaries found in the 2nd House,
or if there are no planets in the House, the Sign on the cusp of the 2nd House.

Let's go swimming . . .

FYI from Ed
Marijuana blocks the Inner Guide Meditation,
and alcohol makes it too unstructured.
Prozac and related drugs are emotionally paralyzing for purposes of this meditation.

Procrastination

If you are procrastinating about something you <u>want</u> to do
or which <u>needs</u> to be started or completed,
meditate with your Wheel of Fortune and Temperance Archetypes:

What steps are necessary to get me to ___?

What is step 1?
What is step 2?

Let's go swimming . . .

CHAPTER TWENTY

MANIFESTATION

One of the many lessons we learn in *The Inner Guide Meditation* relates to manifesting something we want (pages 115, 117). Ed points out that we have to let our Archetypes in on what we're up to in the effort to manifest; otherwise, it is more likely <u>nothing</u> will happen.

Having our goals clearly stated in meditation and in writing is part of what can bring them to fruition. Another important factor is measuring our goals according to what we want to accomplish before we leave this life experience. This works at <u>any</u> age.

The Process
List everything you want to accomplish;
then select the five most urgent goals –
giving yourself the option to revise them at any time.

Within weeks, our manifestation energies bring the first steps toward those goals.

In your daily meditation, include the Archetypes of Houses
2, 5, 8, and 11.

Let them know what you want, and do a circle of hands with these Archetypes.
Balance their energies – feel their energies –
and let your Guide be the one to release hands first.

To track and time your actions,
use the Template for Goal Objectives and Progress (page 149)
and the template for New Moon Cycle Planning and Goal Setting dates and times (page 148).

New Moon Cycle Planning and Goal Setting

(This basic idea came from Laurel Kahaner in "Tarot Nights" Classes.)

As the Moon orbits Earth (a synodic period of 29½ days), and our viewpoint relative to the Sun's direction changes, we see varying slices of the sunlit Moon, which we refer to as Moon phases from New Moon to New Moon. To find out the exact dates and times of the four main Moon phases, use your Astrological Calendar, or see dates for <u>all</u> Moon phases in *Tables of Planetary Phenomenon*.

At each New Moon, draw 8 Tarot cards* for each Moon cycle phase as shown here.

Use the *Tarot-Archetype Essences* (page <u>45-47</u>) in <u>this</u> book for brief interpretations of the Major Arcana and Mary K. Greer's *Tarot for Your Self* for the Major and Minor Arcana, Aces, and Court Cards.

New Moon
Intention/Goal for this New Moon Cycle

Crescent Moon
Foundation for reaching your Intention/Goal

First Quarter Moon
The risk you take to reach the goal

Gibbous Moon
What you must allow in to reach the goal

Full Moon
What has come to fruition and must be integrated
within you to reach your Intention/Goal

Disseminating Moon
What you must share in order to reach the goal

Last Quarter Moon
The responsibility to be taken to reach your Intention/Goal

Balsamic Moon
What you must channel/unleash to reach the goal

*Many people start their New Moon Cycle Planning and Goal Setting by drawing from only the Major Arcana ("Soul" cards) and gradually add the Court cards and Minor Arcana cards, using the entire deck.

Template for Goal Objectives and Progress Dates
Goal Houses
Remember, Goals are wishes until they are written!

Date: _____

Starting with This House/Sign	Counting to 11th Sign and Goal House	Current Objective Of 11th Sign and Goal House	Results or Progress Dates:
1			
2			
3			
4			
5			
6			
7			
8			
9			
10			
11			
12			

Zodiac Sign Goals and Goal Houses
Goals are wishes until they are written!

The Goal of <u>any</u> Sign on your birth chart will be indicated by the 11th <u>Sign</u> from it
(count the first Sign as #1; e.g., the 11th Sign from Aries is Aquarius, etc.):

♈ Aries to Aquarius ♒
♉ Taurus to Pisces ♓
♊ Gemini to Aries ♈
♋ Cancer to Taurus ♉
♌ Leo to Gemini ♊
♍ Virgo to Cancer ♋
♎ Libra to Leo ♌
♏ Scorpio to Virgo ♍
♐ Sagittarius to Libra ♎
♑ Capricorn to Scorpio ♏
♒ Aquarius to Sagittarius ♐
♓ Pisces to Capricorn ♑

The House containing the 11th Sign is the Goal House.

1. Using the Template for *Goal Objectives* (page 149), create your <u>personal</u> template starting with the 1st House Ascendant Sign on <u>your</u> birth chart, and write the Sign next to #1.

2. Leaving the numbers on the template in place, continue around your chart counter-clockwise, and write in only the Signs corresponding next to the House number on the template.

3. Then, write in the 11th Sign from each Sign and its House.

4. Once completed, you have a personal template for writing goals and progress dates.

5. You can now enter notes correlating to each Sign and Goal House from *Brief Sign Energy Influences* (page 152) and *Brief Keywords for Goal Houses* (page 151).

6. As you make progress or complete each Goal, write the dates in the "Result or Progress Date" column.

Brief Keywords for Goal Houses

1   Physical appearance, attitude, habits, starting something new, taking action, personality, general health focus

2   Values, inner resources, talents and income from them, purchases, possessions, bank balances, budgets, wealth, throat health, voice

3   Communications: in your community, with neighbors and with siblings (especially the 1st); short trips, local travel, vehicles, commuting, advertising, writing, broadcasting, early education through high school, student, teaching, criticism, prejudices, dexterity, lungs, vocal cords

4   Residence, property (land and structures), realtors, domestic environment, family, Mother (if your birth was in p.m.), Father (if your birth was in a.m.), emotional foundation, private matters, heritage, results, stomach, digestion

5   Creativity/creative self-expression, romance, pregnancy, births, parenthood, children, friends where there are expectations, income from real estate, entertainment, sports, sporting events, speculation/gambling, heart, back

6   Health of one's body and climactic conditions affecting health, nutrition, disease, hygiene, service providers, work/daily job, working conditions, co-workers/colleagues, laborers, domestic animals, employees, clothing, crafts/crafting

7   Contracts, one-to-one relationships, public relations, roommates, partnerships, matrimony, open enemies

8   Shared material, emotional resources (investments, sex, debts, donations, insurance, taxes, a Will, inheritance)

9   Higher-mind education, foreign affairs, long journey, spiritual practice, philosophy, religion, publishing, horses

10 Career, reputation, employer, Father (if your birth was in p.m.), Mother (if your birth was in a.m.)

11 Manifestation, memberships, groups, alliances, politics, acquaintances, hopes, wishes, long-range goals measured by death

12 Meditation, secrets, secret friends, secret enemies, sleep, hospitals, institutions of confinement, charitable institutions

Brief Sign Energy Influences
As Applied to Your
Sign Goals/Goal Houses

Example
If the 11th Sign is ♈ Aries, you would look at the list on this page for Aries brief keywords to use
toward achieving your goal. Then, look in *Goal Houses* descriptions
for the area of your life where this energy will be directed.

Meditate with the Archetype of the 11th Sign from any other Sign,
asking for assistance in reaching the goal of the 11th Sign in the House where it is placed.

♈ Aries
Being Competitive/Taking Risks/Assertiveness/Being Spontaneous/Showing Independence
♉ Taurus
Determination/Practicality/Endurance/Financial Considerations
♊ Gemini
Optimism/Rational Thinking/Temporary Plans
♋ Cancer
Incremental Progress/Anticipating Results/Nurturing/Being Protective
♌ Leo
Loyalty/Generosity/Dramatic Shift/Choosing the Center of my Actions
♍ Virgo
Methodical/Analyze/Moderation/Being Considerate/Self-Critical/Precise
♎ Libra
Balancing/Basic Fairness/Compromising/Creativity/Using Tact
♏ Scorpio
All or Nothing Efforts/Uncompromising/Using a Business Perspective
♐ Sagittarius
Experimenting/Being more Curious/Companionships/Motivating Others/Confidence/Showing Respect
♑ Capricorn
Calculating Actions/Achieving Tangible Results/Being Responsible/Using Diplomacy/Being Ambitious
♒ Aquarius
Showing Altruism/Objective Detachment/Free Thinking/Showing, Using Originality
♓ Pisces
Being Visionary/Appropriate Sentimentality/Discriminating Sacrifices/
Showing Imagination/Using Wisdom

*Give yourself an Annual *Physical* . . .

Assets:

List 10 things you're good at doing.
Remember, and capitalize on these through your Inner Guide Meditation.
Meditate with the Archetypes related to the appropriate Houses.

Liabilities:

List 10 areas where you need improvement.
One at a time, work on these in your Inner Guide Meditation.
Meditate with the Archetypes related to the appropriate Houses.

*Adapted from **est** workshops

Archetype Focus for the New Year

On the day you celebrate as *New Year's Day*, draw a Major Arcana Tarot card for
"What will (number of the year) bring?"

To manifest that energy,
your "Intention" Archetypes for each monthly New Moon Cycle will support
the Energy Influences of your New Year's Archetype,
and your Archetypes for the rest of each New Moon Cycle
will indicate what must be done to meet your Intention for the monthly New Moon Cycle
to manifest what your New Year's Day Archetype can bring for the year.

Let's go swimming . . .

Gratitude Journal Entries
(an Oprah Winfrey idea)

Gratitude frequently expressed, with as few as 5 entries at each sitting, just naturally invites more for which we can be grateful.

Month, Day, Year

I am grateful . . .

Personal Chart Mandala

Occasionally draw a saucer-sized circle on an 8½ x 11 sheet of paper and <u>in the center</u> put all people and things relating to the 12 Houses listed below that you will automatically allow as your central focus or your "inner circle." Also related to these Houses, <u>outside</u> the circle, put all the people and things allowed in your <u>inner</u> circle "by invitation only." Each time, notice how your priorities change.

Houses and Emphasis

1: Adventures, appearance, physical body, complexion, personal desires, eyes, habits, general health, mannerisms, morality, personal matters, personality, self-interest, temperament/ attitude, worldly outlook

2: Bank balance(s), budget(s), personal debts, earning capacity, income, talent(s), ears, freedom needs, jewelry, precious stones, financial gains, financial losses, profits, loss of profits, neck, throat, ownership rights, possessions, purchasing power, personal resources, shares of stock, voice, vocal chords, wealth

3: Community, community participation, neighbors, neighborhood, communications, advertising, automobile(s), vehicles, visitors, visiting, commuting, early education, gossip, rumors, debates, everyday environment, hands, fingernails, writing, journaling, ghost writing, story-telling, teaching, memory, memories, memorizing, lungs, local travel, short trips, intellect, mentality, informant, literary ability, nerves, prejudices, private thoughts, radio broadcasting, television announcer, reading light literature, receptivity to the ideas of others, school work, shoulders, signature, telephone, vocal organs

4: Family matters, residence, emotional wellbeing, genealogy, stomach, chest, farming, real estate, domestic matters, the environment, estate, home life, private life, parent(s), property, old age, elderly people, digestion

5: Children, creativity, friends where there are expectations, entertainment, fun, games, gambling, sports, romance, heart disease /ailments, hobbies, motion pictures, pregnancy, show business, social affairs, vacation

6: Small and/or domestic animals, disease, illness, hygiene, nutrition, climate-related health issues, job, employees, co-workers, colleagues, physical examination, harvesting, physician, the police, household help, humane societies, tenants

7: Marriage, roommate(s), other partnerships, the general public, rivals, contest, arbitration, litigation/lawsuit, divorce, art, second child, kidney care, peace, peace preservation, union organization

8: Mental regeneration, spiritual regeneration, sex, joint finances, alimony, bankruptcy, inheritance, life insurance, legacies, passion, rebirth, surgery, taxes, making a Will

9: Publishing, writing for publication, higher-mind education, books or other publications, institution of higher learning, philosophy, spirituality, meditation, teaching, ritual, foreign travel, foreign politics, long journey, religion, prayer, preaching, minister, prophet(s), rabbi, attorney, judge, counselor, devotion, virtuous deeds, exploration, foreign trade, international commerce, horse(s), immigration, imports, exports, literature of higher thought, liver care, philanthropy, vision

10: Your reputation, profession, professional status, promotion, public life, fame, employment, social status, popularity, prestige, parent(s), achievement(s), advancement (in life), your employer or supervisor, government service, mastery, high office, famous people, political party in power

11: Acquaintances, goal(s), wishes, benevolence, altruism, a 4th child, membership(s), group participation, civic organization, and politics

12: Meditation, sleep, karma, karmic responsibilities, psychic abilities, charitable organizations, hospital, large organizations, grief, concentration camps, secrets, misfortune, downfall, detective(s), exile, retirement, seclusion, escape, elephants and other large animals, feet, hoax, limitations, losses, oil wells, poverty, prison(er), the sea, slavery, sleepwalking

In a journal, write dates and *"signs"* showing you're *tapped in*
to the Energy Influences of your Archetypes.
Looking back on these is fun, interesting, and affirming of your IGM process.

CHAPTER TWENTY-ONE

THE PATH OF SELF-CULTIVATION

The Fundamental Path of a Plain Good Life
From the I Ching *Book of Changes*
(Pages 167-182)

1
To follow nature, or to cultivate and regulate oneself,
is the fundamental path of life.

2
Centeredness is the greatest source of the universe.
Balance is the underlying principle of all things.
Therefore, the attainment of inner centeredness and balance.

11
The path of self-cultivation starts with the
"ordinariness" of human life.
Its extensiveness is revealed through everything in the universe.

12
One of self-cultivation extends his/her awareness
To know people and correct himself/herself.

14
Self-cultivation also resembles beginning a long journey
or climbing a mountain.

16
With sincerity, one can find the way.

17
To be sincere means to choose the right way
And stay with it persistently.
When one is sincere, her/his mind is clear.
When one's mind is clear, she/he is naturally sincere.

Transformation and Possibility
Rather than having things be as they are, have them be as *transformation*.

That was one of the many ideas on personal transformation taught in the **est** training created by Werner Erhard, founder of **est** (1971). Some of the following thoughts are adapted from 1988 **est** workshops and are useful in working with personal transits through our Archetypes.

To keep thriving in personal growth,
shift feelings of being "important" or "unimportant"
to responsible *actions*.
Either way, get <u>over</u> yourself!
Go for Greater!

Laying new track:
- Does "possibility" show up in your thoughts? – in your world? – in thoughts about your future?
- When we speak and listen from "possibility," we <u>create</u> it in "now" time. It's not a concept, and it doesn't exist otherwise.
- <u>Be</u> a stand for possibility.
- Working with your transits on a daily basis, through your Archetypes, you have the opportunity to speak and listen from "possibility."

Languaging the new track:
- Given my history and my circumstances, what commitment can I make or what stand can I take?
- Knowing what my birth chart/blueprint shows I am here to experience, can I take a stand for the "free will" to expand on "possibility" in favor of contribution to the good of <u>all</u> and leave behind the possibility of fear or inadequacy or . . .?

Living from Possibility:
- Ask your Fool Archetype to show you the possibilities when you take a stand for <u>un</u>comfortable, <u>un</u>predictable, and stepping into the <u>un</u>known.
- Meditate with the Archetypes of your transits to take you on the adventure of "transformation."

Tree of Life
Exercise, Attributes, and Connections

Symbolically, the Tree of Life represents the force necessary to unite opposites within ourselves toward spiritual transformation, as further explained in *Kabbalah* by Charles Poncé, pages 148-150. The Tree of Life dates from the 11ᵗʰ Century in France. Its 32 Paths of Wisdom are related to the chakras and Kundalini yoga, astrological values, and Tarot, and its 10 planetary spheres represent energies not available to our ordinary perceptions on the material plane but which are available in meditation (see Sefirah Attributes on page 164 of <u>this</u> book).

The Tree of Life reinvigorates our spiritual quest with mysticism by identifying building blocks of the Universe in ourselves (as shown on the Sefirah list). Disconnections can occur because of childhood criticism or other unfortunate occurrences. We may use our heads more than our feelings; conversely, we may not set boundaries and lose our<u>selves</u> in loving others. We may not keep our word, or we may not trust others to keep theirs. Someone may be vulnerable to an abusive relationship or co-dependency. We may never have experienced the joy of pure creativity for a multitude of reasons.

Using the exercise on page 163 with the IGM is an opportunity to achieve wholeness by healing the disconnected aspects of our Tree through our Archetypes and transits.* We can then acknowledge our power on the Inner Plane and come closer and closer to Center through the meditation to express it on the Outer Plane. In *The Inner Guide Meditation*, on pages 242-243, Ed introduces an excellent exercise using the "Spheres/Sephirot" of a different system for use with the Tree of Life when we first begin the IGM work.

From this exercise, we can see where we need to meditate for development of disconnected attributes throughout life in alignment with our astrological birth chart indications. Connected triads indicate completions in mental power, moral power, and creative power.

*The basic idea of the exercise (unrelated to the IGM) used here is based on a lecture at the 2012 United Astrology Conference by noted Astrologer, Maureen Ambrose. In-depth study may be obtained through www.kabbalahsociety.org as well as books noted in *Additional Reading Opportunities* (Appendix).

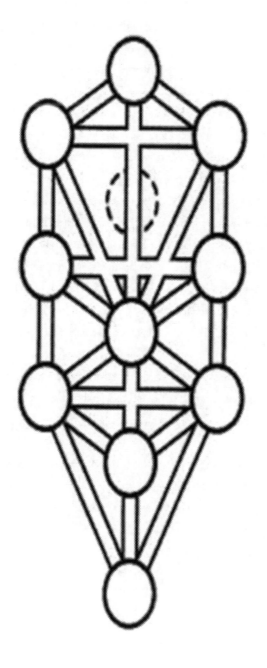

TREE OF LIFE

Tree of Life Exercise

On the Tree of Life template on page 162, write the Sign of your Ascendant (ASC), the symbols and Signs for your Sun (☉), Moon (☽) and planets Mercury (☿), Venus (♀), Mars (♂), Jupiter (♃), Saturn (♄), Pluto (♇), Uranus (♅), and Neptune (♆) with their Signs and Houses from your birth chart where indicated according to the Sefirah Attributes list on page 164 (1 being at the top and 10 being at the bottom of the Tree), without adding the degrees or counting orbs. Note that the broken circle is Daat/Pluto.

Draw lines between the connections by Sign, if they exist: ♂ (conjunction), ✷ (sextile), ☐ (square), △ (trine), or ♂ (opposition) as shown on the *Zodiac Sign Connections*, page 165, and see the indications of attributes/Archetypes and *Birth Chart House Attributes* above the connections table.

Meditate with the Archetypes where there are *disconnections* for healing of your spiritual energy related to the specific attributes.

Sefirah Attributes

Hebrew	Sefirah	Attributes	Related Planet	Archetype
Keter	1	Crown of Knowledge/Spirit	Neptune	Hanged Man
Chokhmah	2	Wisdom/Insight Active Intellect	Uranus	Fool
Binah	3	Unfolding of Intelligence/Intuition Passive Intellect	Saturn	World
Chesed	4	Expansion of Will Mercy/Active Emotion	Jupiter	Wheel of Fortune
Gevurah	5	Power/ Passive Emotion	Mars	Tower
Tiferet	6	Harmony/Balance	Sun	Sun
Netzach	7	Victory/Active Psycho-Bio Process	Venus	Empress
Hod	8	Majesty/Glory Passive-Bio Thought Process	Mercury	Magician
Yesod	9	Oneness/Feeling Realization Foundation	Moon	Moon (not your personal Moon)
Malkhut	10	Personality/Body Kingdom Earth	Ascendant	Archetype of Sign on the Ascendant/ 1st House cusp

Birth Chart House Attributes
(For Use with the Tree of Life Exercise)

1 Body, Personality, Ego
2 Talents, Values, Possessions
3 Siblings, Early Education, Communication
4 Roots, Emotional Security, Mother, Residence, Family
5 Creativity, Children, Love Given, Friends, Play
6 Health, Service Given, Service Received, Pets
7 Other People, Partnerships, Shadows, Open Enemies
8 Shared Resources – Emotional and Material
9 Higher-Mind Consciousness, Spirituality, Religion, Philosophy
10 Career, Reputation, Status, Father, Authority Figures
11 Goals, Manifestation, Group Acquaintances, Love Received
12 Hidden Strengths, Hidden Enemies

Zodiac Sign Connections

	Conjunction	Sextile	Square	Trine	Opposition
♈	Aries–Aries	Aries–Gemini	Aries–Cancer	Aries–Leo	Aries–Libra
♉	Taurus–Taurus	Taurus–Cancer	Taurus–Leo	Taurus–Virgo	Taurus–Scorpio
♊	Gemini–Gemini	Gemini–Leo	Gemini–Virgo	Gemini–Libra	Gemini–Sagittarius
♋	Cancer–Cancer	Cancer–Virgo	Cancer–Libra	Cancer–Scorpio	Cancer–Capricorn
♌	Leo–Leo	Leo–Libra	Leo–Scorpio	Leo–Sagittarius	Leo–Aquarius
♍	Virgo–Virgo	Virgo–Scorpio	Virgo–Sagittarius	Virgo–Capricorn	Virgo–Pisces
♎	Libra–Libra	Libra–Sagittarius	Libra–Capricorn	Libra–Aquarius	Libra–Aries
♏	Scorpio–Scorpio	Scorpio–Capricorn	Scorpio–Aquarius	Scorpio–Pisces	Scorpio–Taurus
♐	Sagittarius–Sagittarius	Sagittarius–Aquarius	Sagittarius–Pisces	Sagittarius–Aries	Sagittarius–Gemini
♑	Capricorn–Capricorn	Capricorn–Pisces	Capricorn–Aries	Capricorn–Taurus	Capricorn–Cancer
♒	Aquarius–Aquarius	Aquarius–Aries	Aquarius–Taurus	Aquarius–Gemini	Aquarius–Leo
♓	Pisces–Pisces	Pisces–Taurus	Pisces–Gemini	Pisces–Cancer	Pisces–Virgo

Dwell on the rewards of success,
not the penalties of failure.

Good fortune comes from the wisdom developed
through understanding one's past.
Lu, Hexagram #10, Line 5

Lasting change can be effected only when the <u>need</u> for change is understood and internalized.
The incentive or reward must be interpreted and internalized.
Move in the direction of your goals without fear until they're set!
Denis Waitley

Know your Feng Shui *Auspicious Directions*
and
your Chinese birth animal.

CHAPTER TWENTY-TWO

CONSTANTLY TAKE IN YOUR ESSENTIAL ENERGIES

When you don't have an affinity for one or more of your Archetypes . . .
remember, our Archetypes are the life energies that *pour* out of each of us.

They have to be in balance on our Inner Plane for harmony to exist on our Outer Plane.
(Additional information is found in Ed's book on pages 6 and 7.)

The possibilities are legion for why you may not have an affinity for one or more of your Archetypes; however, consider the following:

- Be sure you've met the Archetype and have asked the First Questions.
- Ask your Guide to confirm that the figure is a true guide on your Inner Plane.
- Confirm with your Guide that you should accept the gift offered by the figure.
- If all of that is confirmed, also be sure to revisit your writing of her or his original appearance at your first meeting, and consider whether your personal growth through the meditation has also affected the growth and appearance of the Archetype.
- If you are uncomfortable about the current discussion you need to have with this Archetype, ask your Guide to assist you in communicating with him or her.
- Learning to use your personal transits for meeting with the correct Archetypes strengthens your bond with them. The keywords in this book represent the basic energies associated with the Archetypes of the zodiacal signs, planets, and luminaries. Your own Archetypes have "personalities" that emanate from <u>you</u>.
- Be sure you're meditating with your Archetypes on a regular basis, even when things are going along very well on the Outer Plane. In fact, if that is the case, thank them, and ask them to "Bring it on!"
- If things are not as they should be on the <u>Outer</u> Plane, remember, our Archetypes love us enough to tell us the truth, and it may not be what we want to hear. Through your transits, you will *hear* what they are trying to tell you. Are you giving them permission to affect your thinking?
- Ask your Guide whether you are receiving the information you need from a particular Archetype.
- Ask yourself whether they represent parts of *yourself* for which you have no affinity.
- Do an I Ching toss asking for the hexagram that best describes how you should use the advice given.
- If you are having a meditation issue – take the issue to your Guide. Tell him what's going on, and ask his advice.

Working with your Archetypes through your transits will help you
hear and heed
what your Archetypes <u>need you to know</u>,
and your relationship with them will grow.

Live your life out of your promise *and* with purpose.
<u>Intervene</u> when your desires are not what your promises are!
est Aphorisms

When your Outer reality creates distraction,
go immediately to your *Inner* reality to *re-create* your <u>own</u> Outer reality!

Re-create yourself,
by constantly taking in your *Essential Energy* at your brain pool.

Good Mother Messages

Once you've <u>met</u> your Lunar Construct/Inner Mother,
consider the Archetype Tarot cards you draw for this exercise to be messages from her.

(Adapted from the original creation of
Jack L. Rosenberg, Ph.D., as taught
by Laurel Kahaner, 1996)

This exercise can be incorporated into your regular IGM sessions, as confirmation from your Inner Mother after your Daily Moon Meditations, especially if the Daily Moon is an Archetype drawn for one of the statements listed below. They can also be reassuring in your New Moon Cycle Planning and Goal Setting if one of the Archetypes you draw is among them.

Using only the Major Arcana, draw one Archetype for each statement. Set each card aside until all have been drawn, and at the bottom of the confirmation list, you will note a question to ask and to draw the response from these Archetypal representations you have set aside. Then, next to each phrase, write the name of the Archetype and general keywords most closely associated with the confirmation phrase as suggested in the *Tarot-Archetype Essences* (page 45-47).

Which Archetype confirms that

. . . you love me;

. . . I am a "wanted" child;

. . . I'm "special" to <u>you</u>;

. . . you <u>see</u> and <u>hear</u> me;

. . . it's not what I <u>do</u> but who I <u>am</u> that you love;

. . . you love me <u>and</u> give me permission to be different from you in all ways I choose;

. . . you'll <u>always</u> take care of me;

. . . you'll <u>always</u> be there/available for me;

. . . I'll never be alone;

. . . I can <u>always</u> trust you;

. . . I can <u>always</u> trust my Inner Guide and Archetypes, knowing they're ready to help me when I ask;

. . . you'll say "no" to me (block my effort) <u>because</u> you love me, and if I need an explanation, all I need to do is ask, and you'll respond;

. . . I don't ever have to "fear" – or be afraid – again;

. . . your love will always heal my inner pain/hurt.

From the cards you drew for the above confirmations, shuffle those and draw an Archetype for this question to Good Mother: **Which Archetype most represents what you want me to never forget?**

Can't get to sleep?

Without analyzing it beyond reason, sometimes
it's a simple matter of a Personal Void of Course Moon.

Ask your Pisces Archetype (Moon)
To help you set up a
"Sleeping Lodge"
in your Inner Landscape.

Then, when you are feeling restless and
have difficulty getting to sleep,
go with your Guide to the Moon Sleeping Lodge.

(Once there, if you ask, you may even get a massage.)

CHAPTER TWENTY-THREE

THE BOTTOM LINE . . .

You now have your IGM tools and New Moon Planning and Goal Setting tool
for your basic intention each month.

Live on the *Outer* Plane from your *Inner* Plane.
Get out of your own way!
Take a deep breath – nod your head "yes"
and keep moving forward – remembering that you <u>chose</u> it!

On the one hand, through personal daily transits, your Archetypes <u>may</u> tell you what you <u>*want*</u> to hear; on the other hand, through your <u>transits</u>, they tell you what you <u>*need*</u> to hear, and if you look ahead, they can also help you *shift* energy! Transits will always play out one way or the other, and they activate your Archetypes. The key is awareness <u>and</u> working with your Archetypes to shift "unpleasant" or "upsetting" transits to a higher vibration of opportunity – whether that means learning or <u>doing</u> or both.

Nurture your Inner Life, your Outer Body, and the Earth.
There has to be a willingness to <u>do</u> the work, to take the spiritually superior approach,
which – oh by the way – will likely also bring a superior result!

Keep up with *yourself!*
When negativity creeps in, examine what role it's playing . . . when that role is no longer needed,
replace it with something that opens the door for creative change in your life
<u>and</u> for the good of all, with no detriment to you.
Every time negativity shows up to your *party*, go to your Brain Pool Circle of Hands until it leaves.

<u>Become</u> *time*! Make every moment purposeful.
Cultivate the virtues of purity, responsibility, innocence (based on knowledge), modesty, moderation, integrity, intention, creativity, perseverance, and receptivity to the wisdom of your Archetypes through IGM – even when you've reached a modicum of satisfaction with your life.

Constantly take in <u>your</u> *Essential Energies.*
Speak <u>with</u> others by expressing <u>your</u> *true* point of view,
based on your experience of a situation and/or individual.
Choose your *virtue* over saying negative <u>facts</u> about someone.
Remember, *violence* <u>includes</u> toxic talk about others.
Choose <u>only</u> extraordinary relationships that mirror your self-worth.
Bring "Good Will" wherever you go. Make a difference! Perfect how you show up! Perfect how you *operate.*

You now also <u>have</u> the spiritually-confirming Energy of the I Ching
in combination with your vote on your Board of Directors/Basic Archetypes.

You have sublime assurance you're on the "right track."

Integrate it all into yourself to reach your Center.

In cultivating the *Integral Way,* one cultivates the virtue of self-integration.
To be integral is to be one with the true, deep nature of the universal origin.
Chung Fu #61 Commentary on *Reality*

. . . Re-wire your brain!

You *get* it – right?
This is what's <u>so</u>!

<u>I</u> know – "so what?"
<u>So</u> – you now have a way to organize your IGM toolbox.
Keep learning how to <u>use</u> it all –
No holding back.
Make a difference!

Wrap your brain around and tap into these sustainable *Energy Influences*.

Use
IGM
Astrological Calendar/Transits
New Moon Planning and Goal Setting
Good Mother Messages
I Ching
Numerology
Tarot

<u>Take</u> the time – <u>schedule</u> it –
<u>do</u> the work!

Take the ultimate *get-away* <u>every</u> day!

Go *Swimming in Your Brain* . . .

APPENDIX

And This Word Means What?

Accidental Detriment

When the Sun, Moon, or a planet is in the House opposite the House of its own Accidental Rulership, its natural basic expression is limited.

Accidental Exaltation

The Sun, Moon, or planet is in the House "Ruled" by the Exalted Sign.

Accidental Fall

The Sun, Moon, or planet in a House opposite the House of its Accidental Exaltation, is said to be in Accidental Fall – its most debilitated, confined, and weakened placement.

Accidental Rulership

Refers to the House a planet rules (see Ruler). Where a planet might be in the House it rules, it is not in the Sign it rules. For example, the Sun may be in the 5th House (where it Rules) but in the Sign of Aries (which it does not Rule).

Adept

Someone in the IGM system who (once brought to consciousness) has expertise in certain matters pertaining to one of the Elements (Fire, Earth, Air, Water) and the Houses under rulership of the Element; e.g., the Fire element rules Houses 1, 5, and 9 (on a flat chart) pertaining generally to appearance, initiation, children, creativity, performing, philosophy, higher education, foreign travel, or spirituality.

The Adept is someone with planets, Sun, Moon, or Ascendant without one Element or Quality. By the above example, without planets, the Sun, Moon, or Ascendant in Fire Signs, Aries (Cardinal Fire), Leo (Fixed Fire), or Sagittarius (Mutable Fire) the individual would be a **Fire Adept**, an expert in Houses 1, 5, and 9. The **Earth Adept** is someone whose planets, Sun, Moon, or Ascendant are not in Earth Signs, Taurus (Fixed Earth), Virgo (Mutable Earth), or Capricorn (Cardinal Earth), and whose expertise would be in Houses 2, 6, and 10. The **Air Adept** is an individual without planets, the Sun, Moon, or Ascendant in Air Signs: Aquarius (Fixed Air), Gemini (Mutuable Air), Libra (Cardinal Air), and would have expertise in Houses 3, 7, and 11. The **Water Adept** would be someone without planets, the Sun, Moon, or Ascendant in Water Signs: Cancer, Scorpio, or Pisces. His/her expertise would be in Houses, 4, 8, and 12.

AFGO	Street slang for "Another Friggin' Growth Opportunity" – as in, not something we really want to experience but which <u>does</u> contribute to one's personal growth!

Alien Energy Constructs	In the IGM system, these patterns represent specific planetary, Sun, and/or Moon placements and unions in a birth chart which are conjunct the Ascendant, Sun, or Moon. Except for their areas of expertise, the Alien Energy Constructs often have great difficulty with conventional lifestyles. (See also *The Inner Guide Meditation*, pages 217-228.) The individuals include **Alien Powers** (<u>Sun</u> conjunct Saturn, Uranus, Neptune, or Pluto within orb of 15°+/-). The **Saturnian Power** is one whose energy brings to form and stabilizes by focusing her/his attention on whomever or whatever . The **Uranian Power** is non-judgmental and often a genius in the use of their multi-level awareness. A **Neptunian Power** is the "illusion-maker" through a natural ability in the arts and clairvoyance. One who is a **Plutonian Power** is the natural sleuth and "remodeler" of the Universe through their charisma in relating to the masses. **Alien Vessels** (<u>Moon</u> conjunct Saturn, Uranus, Neptune, or Pluto within orb of 12°+/-). The **Saturnian Vessel** brings stability and organization to those around them, as well as inspires practical, Earth-plane ideas. A **Uranian Vessel** can bring groups together in friendly cooperation, as well as inspire ideas in astrology and innovation. The **Neptunian Vessel** is profoundly psychic and can inspire compassion, sympathy, and deep mystical feelings. The **Plutonian Vessel** has the ability to free any *blocked* energy in others, and they have great charisma, sleuthing, and healing powers. **Alien Instruments** (Saturn, Uranus, Neptune, or Pluto within orb of 10°+/-) conjunct the Ascendant, in the 1st House or 12th House. These individuals function as *broadcasters, amplifiers, and receivers* of one of the following planetary energies in people around them. The **Saturnian Instrument** is the *tester and guardian* of humanity related to time, space, form, secrets of geometry, stability, and safety. A **Uranian Instrument** broadcasts, amplifies, and receives energy related to sister/brotherhood, freedom, genius, altruism, and invention. One who is a **Neptunian Instrument** needs periodic physical privacy to stay centered; they are light-sensitive and must protect their eyes. This individual broadcasts and amplifies energy related to sensitivity, sympathy, music, poetry, clairvoyance and psychic ability. **Mixed Patterns** are generally due to mutual reception; such as, Saturn in Cancer and the Moon in Capricorn (a mutual reception Saturnian Vessel) with the ability to function interchangeably between them.

Alien Patterns	See "Alien Energy Constructs" above.
Angles	The Angular Houses are 1, 4, 7, and 10; each 90° from one to the next in the horoscope, and we can speak of them as the *chart angles*.
ASAP	As soon as possible.
Ascendant	ASC is the degree and *Sign* on the dividing line (cusp) of the 1st House (on the eastern Horizon) of a horoscopic chart. It is often spoken of interchangeably as someone's "*Rising Sign*" degree.
Aspects	The degree relationship/connection between one planet and one or more other planets, the Sun, Moon, Ascendant, Mid-Heaven, Chiron, or the asteroids. The aspects used in this book include the conjunction ☌ (0°+7°), sextile ✳ (60° within orb of 5°+/-), quintile Q (72° within orb of 3°+/-), square ☐ (90° within orb of 7°+/-), trine △ (120° within orb of 7°+/-), and opposition ☍ (180° within orb of 7°+/-). See "Orb" below. (See also *The Arkana Dictionary of Astrology* by Fred Gettings.)
Cardinal	One of three "quadruplicities" (Cardinal, Fixed, Mutable) indicating the qualities of the 12 *Signs* through which the four Elements find expression. *Cardinal Signs* are Aries ♈, Cancer ♋, Libra ♎, and Capricorn ♑. They initiate action and lead. This is active energy in Houses 1, 4, 7, and 10 that moves forward and upward on a "Flat" chart, and their energies (initiative, active, movable, lead) influence those Houses regardless of what *Sign* is in a native's chart.
Chakras	Seven vortexes, each alternately called "an energy wheel," containing subtle centers distributed in five circles over the length of the middle channel of the human body and are crisscrossed by the two most powerful of all psychic energy life forces, Ida and Pingala. These are combined into Kundalini energy and starting from the lower spine coil upward around the spine and vortexes like snakes. Each chakra wheel is viewed as a consciousness center relating to specific aspects of human behavior and development. (See *Bodymind* by Kenneth Dychtwald, pages 84-87.)

Conjunction ☌	Two or more planets in the same Sign within 7° of each other. This energy is very powerful, and the closer the orb, the more prominent the union. Whether the energy of the conjunction is compatible or not depends upon the Sign and placement of the planet, Sun, or Moon in the horoscope.
CRF	Consciousness Resistant Factor (pages 21-23), is a cosmic energy in some natal charts that was pushed into the darkness of unconsciousness of the individual at birth. Until <u>un</u>blocked and consistently conscious, there is more hardship in that area of one's life, and the talents and abilities represented by these Energy Influences are blocked and otherwise projected onto others. There can be zero or many CRFs in a birth chart.
C r F	Consciousness Receptive Factor – the previously blocked energy is unblocked, and the Archetype is receptive to participation with all the other Archetypes toward manifesting the talents and abilities she or he represents in an individual.
Cusp	The dividing line between the Houses of a horoscope in the House system used for this book. It can also refer to the end of the last degree of one Sign as it moves into the beginning of the first degree of the next Sign; e.g., Aries 29°35'25" and Taurus 00°33'59".
Decan	Used interchangeably with "*Decanate.*" An astrological Sign has 30° and is divided into three 10° arcs referred to as decans. Each decan shows the purpose of the Sign (1st=physical; 2nd=mental; and 3rd =spiritual). A decan is effectively the receiver of a Sign's projection. See "Dwad" below.
Detriment	When a planet is in *detriment* it isn't necessarily weak, but it is *limited* in the basic expression of its characteristics.
Direct Motion	Actual motion of the planets when not in Retrograde. For example, Saturn takes 30 years to move through the 12 Signs of the Zodiac, including retrograde and direct motion; the Sun revolves around the Earth over one year, advancing through the 12 Signs at a pace of 1° a day, starting with 0°. The motion of each planet is different, and *transits* are based upon their individual motion. (See *Transits* below.)

Dwad	The dwad suggests one's approach to achieving the purpose shown by the decan. A Sign has 30° divided by 12 into arcs of 2 ½°. They are interpreted according to the Sign Ruler and House.
Elements	Fire, Earth, Air, and Water – Signs are also grouped into four triplicities, which relate to tendencies in temperament: **Fire** (the fastest) correlates to Aries, Leo, and Sagittarius and the masculine Houses of Life 1, 5, and 9. **Earth** (the most grounded) relates to Taurus, Virgo, and Capricorn and the feminine Houses of Substance, 2, 6, and 10. **Air** (mental) is connected with Gemini, Libra, and Aquarius and the masculine relationship Houses 3, 7, and 11. **Water** (emotions/feelings) relates to Cancer, Scorpio, and Pisces and the feminine Houses of endings and the unconscious, 4, 8, and 12. A preponderance of planets found in Signs belonging to one of these is a major factor in the person's quality of expression in some phase of her or his life.
Ephemeris	Usually a book of degree tables showing the degrees of movement by the Sun, North Node, and planets based upon Ephemeris Time in some cases and Noon Greenwich Mean Time in other cases. Ephemerides give additional useful information for Astrologers. An ephemeris is also often found in the back of an Astrological Calendar.
est	Erhard Seminar Training. A personal transformational movement founded in 1971 by Werner Erhard. It is based upon achieving *wholeness* or *completion* – truth, a purpose of life in which one is "complete" in relation to self, others, and the Universe. (See Additional Reading below for "Werner Erhard.")
Exalted	A planet in a Sign harmonious with its own nature is said to be in *exaltation* and quite beneficial, and in Manly P. Hall's *Astrological Keywords,* promises the native excellence in the qualities represented by the planet and Sign.

Fixed	One of three "quadruplicities" (Cardinal, Fixed, Mutable) indicating the qualities of the 12 Signs through which the four Elements find expression. *Fixed* Signs are Taurus ♉, Leo ♌, Scorpio ♏, and Aquarius ♒, the related Houses of which are 2, 5, 8, and 11 on a Flat chart, and their energies (persistent, reliable, resourceful, resistant, restrictive) influence those Houses regardless of the Sign in a native's chart. Fixed signs are durable, and their movement has a stair-step, lasting effect with no going back – like a sudden change that plateaus.
Flat Chart/Natural Chart	The Ascendant is in Aries, and the Houses follow unintercepted around the Horoscope in successive Signs; whereas, one's personal natal chart will not necessarily have Aries on the Ascendant.
Greenwich Mean Time (GMT)	Local mean time in Greenwich, England, which is on the zero line of longitude.
Horary	The branch of Astrology that answers "burning" questions by a querent according to the specific time of the question or time at which the Astrologer *understands* the question. These would not be casual questions of mere curiosity. (See *The Martial Arts of Horary* by J. Lee Lehman, Ph.D.)
Horoscope	In modern Western Astrology, a Horoscope is a circular chart erected with the Ascendant on the cusp of the 1st House (East/left) and a total of 12 Houses, used to study someone's individuality.
Interception	Refers to a Sign posited between two cusps of a House and is indicative of a wider sphere of influence within that House inasmuch as there are three Signs (and conceivably planets and/or luminaries with all three Signs inside the House).
Kundalini	Deep enfoldment and empowerment lodged at the base of one's spine waiting to be awakened. (See *The Inner Guide Meditation*, pages 74-91.)
Mercury Retrograde	(☿ ℞) (See pages 101-109.) Mercury appears to be going backwards against the backdrop of fixed stars – like a vehicle on the freeway passing a train going the opposite direction. Astrologically and physiologically, it can interfere with communications at every level – as in slower.

Mutable	One of three "quadruplicities" (Cardinal, Fixed, Mutable) indicating the qualities of the 12 Signs through which the four Elements find expression. *Mutable* signs are Gemini Ⅱ, Virgo ♍, Sagittarius ♐, and Pisces ♓ influencing Houses 3, 6, 9, and 12 on a Flat chart, and their energies (changeability, adaptability, instability) influence those Houses regardless of what Sign is in a native's chart. The effect of the Energy Influences on the Mutable signs looks like three steps forward and up with two steps back and down, going over and over the same steps.
Natal	Birth (from the Latin *natus*). A natal chart indicates by aspects the influence of the planets, luminaries, and Signs on the life of an individual.
Native	The individual about whom a natal chart is cast.
Opposition ☍	A 180° aspect between two celestial bodies opposite each other within a +/-7° orb (used in this book).
Orb	For purposes of this book, an orb signifies the degrees within which an aspect has influence as between two planets or luminaries in a horoscope or as used in transits between the celestial bodies.
Posited	Placed. In <u>this</u> book, the term refers to where a celestial body is placed in an astrological chart.
Projection	Defense mechanism; our *reaction* to a trait we attribute to someone else that is likely our own.
Quadruplicity	Used interchangeably with Quality.
Quality	Refers to each group of four Zodiac signs: Cardinal, Fixed, or Mutable quadruplicities – the common nature attributed to each group among all 12 Signs and by which the Elements (Fire, Earth, Air, and Water) each find expression.
Quintile **Q**	An aspect of 72° between two celestial bodies that denotes *exceptional* talent.
Radix	The horoscope of birth or the *root* for delineating a horoscopic chart.

Retrograde	Signified by **R**, which is applied to planetary symbols periodically when a planet appears to move backward against the backdrop of the stars along the Zodiac belt. The effect on us humans is a slowing down on the action of the planet in the area shown in our birth charts and is otherwise different for each of us, according to the planet, Sign, and House.
Ruler	The Ruler of a Sign, House, or planet, the Sun or Moon confers greater power to embody and/or fulfill its characteristics and carry its influence throughout one's natal chart.
Sextile ✳	A 60° aspect of opportunity to be consciously utilized between the planets and/or luminaries involved in the aspect by birth and transit.
Square ☐	The square (90°) between two planets and/or luminaries brings considerable challenges, which can also serve to spur us to action and bring favorable results.
Transits	The Sun, Moon, planets, Chiron, the S. Node and N. Node are the celestial bodies referred to in this book. They *transit* the Signs, and an ephemeris is used to track their movement. See discussion relative to the IGM starting on page 80.
Triggers	Triggers create the environment for aspects to manifest their Energy Influences. An example is the Taurus Moon on July 29, 2013, which triggered a Grand Sextile of 60° each among the Moon, Jupiter/Mars, Venus, Saturn, Pluto, and Neptune.
Trine △	A beneficial aspect of 120° among three planets and/or the Moon and/or the Sun.
Zodiacal Belt	The entire circle <u>in</u> which your Sun, Moon, and planets are situated is your "Horoscope." The "path" <u>on</u> which Sign degrees are placed <u>around</u> your horoscope is the "zodiacal belt." This can be understood to be an invisible path/belt on the ecliptic along which the constellations (with zodiacal signs) move by degrees (0-29).

Additional Reading Opportunities
According to One's Meditation Level

Starting Out

The Inner Guide Meditation – A Spiritual Technique for the 21st Century by Edwin C. Steinbrecher,
Revised 6th Edition, Samuel Weiser, York Beach ME, 1989.

The Book of Changes and the Unchanging Truth by Taoist Master Ni, Hua Ching,
The Shrine of the Eternal Breath of Tao, Malibu, CA, and
College of Tao and Traditional Chinese Healing, Los Angeles, CA 1983.

Owning Your Own Shadow by Robert A. Johnson, HarperCollins, San Francisco CA, 1993.

Pocket Astrologer by Jim Maynard, Quicksilver Productions.com.

Tarot for Your Self by Mary K. Greer, Newcastle Publishing Co., N. Hollywood CA, 1984.

Transits – The Time of Your Life by Betty Lunsted, Samuel Weiser, Inc., York Beach ME, 1980.

Advancing, Level 1

The Inner Guide Meditation – A Spiritual Technique for the 21st Century by Edwin C. Steinbrecher,
Revised 6th Edition, Samuel Weiser, York Beach ME, 1989.

Pocket Astrologer by Jim Maynard, Quicksilver Productions.com.

Celestial Guide (Appointment Calendar) by Jim Maynard, Quicksilver Productions.com.

Tarot for Your Self by Mary K. Greer, Newcastle Publishing Co., N. Hollywood CA, 1984.

Planets in Transit by Robert Hand, Expanded 2nd Edition, Revised, Whitford Press,
Atglen PA, 2001.

Karmic Astrology Retrogrades and Reincarnation, Vol. II, by Martin Schulman, Samuel Weiser, Inc.,
York Beach ME, 1977.

Owning Your Own Shadow by Robert A. Johnson, HarperCollins, San Francisco CA, 1993.

Advancing, Level 2

The Inner Guide Meditation: A Spiritual Technique for the 21st Century by Edwin C. Steinbrecher,
Revised 6th Edition, Samuel Weiser, York Beach ME, 1989.

Pocket Astrologer by Jim Maynard, Quicksilver Productions.com.

Celestial Guide (Appointment Calendar) by Jim Maynard, Quicksilver Productions.com.

Tarot for Your Self by Mary K. Greer, Newcastle Publishing Co., N. Hollywood CA, 1984.

Planets in Transit by Robert Hand, Expanded 2nd Edition, Revised, Whitford Press,
Atglen PA, 2001.

Karmic Astrology Retrogrades and Reincarnation, Vol. II, by Martin Schulman,
Samuel Weiser, Inc., York Beach ME, 1977.

The American Ephemeris for the 21st Century 2000-2050 at Midnight, ACS.

Tables of Planetary Phenomena by Neil F. Michelsen, 2nd Edition, ACS, San Diego CA, 1995.

Chiron and the Healing Journey by Melanie Reinhart, Penguin Books,
Harmondsworth, Middlesex, England, 1989.

Pertinent Books for Further Reference

Astrological Keywords by Manly P. Hall, Philosophical Research Society, Los Angeles CA, 1973.

Astrology – The Evidence of Science, Percy Seymour, Arkana, Penguin, London, 1990.

Bodymind by Kenneth Dychtwald, Ph.D., (pages 84-87) Pantheon Books/Random House, New York, 1977.

Daodejing: Its Editions and Versions, ISBN 978 -7-80123-862-7.

Decanates by Bernice Prill Grebner, AFA, 1980.

Earth Cycles – The Scientific Evidence for Astrology, Vol. 1 The Physical Sciences, compiled/edited by Valerie Vaughan, One Reed Publications, Amherst MA, 2002.

Easy-to-use Feng Shui by Lillian Too, Collins & Brown Ltd., London, 1999.

Essential Dignities by J. Lee Lehman, Ph.D., Whitford Press, Atglen PA, 1981.

Horoscope Symbols by Robert Hand, Whitford Press, Atglen PA, 1981.

Jung on Synchronicity and the Paranormal, Princeton University Press, 1997.

Kabbalah – An Introduction and Illumination for the World Today by Charles Poncé, 2nd Quest Edition, Theosophical Publishing, Straight Arrow Books, San Francisco CA ,1980.

Man and his Symbols, by Carl G. Jung, M.-L. von Franz, and Aldus Editors, Aldus Books Ltd., London 1964.

Retrograde Planets by Erin Sullivan, Arkana Penguin Books, London, 1992.

Sefer Yetzirah, The Book of Creation – In Theory and Practice, by Aryeh Kaplan, Revised Edition, Weiser Books, York Beach ME, 1977.

The Anatomy of Fate – Kabbalistic Astrology by Z'ev ben Shimon Halevi, 1st American Paperback Edition, Samuel Weiser, York Beach ME, 1987.

The Arkana Dictionary of Astrology by Fred Gettings, Arkana Penguin Books, 1985.

The Dynamic Universe by Theodore P. Snow, 3rd Edition, West Publishing Co., 1987.

The Essential Jung, Selected Writings, Princeton University Press, 1983.

The Illustrated Book of Laozi by Zhou Chuncai, New World Press, Beijing, China, ISBN 978-7-80228-592-7.

The Inner Teachings of Taoism by Chang Po-Tuan, Shambhala Publications, 2001.

The Kabbalistic Tree of Life – Kabbalistic Metaphysics by Z'ev ben Shimon Halevi, Revised Edition, Kabbalah Society, 2009.

The Martial Arts of Horary by J. Lee Lehman, Ph.D., Whitford Press, Atglen PA, 2002.

The Numerology Kit by Carol Adrienne, Penguin Books, 1988.

The Rulership Book by Rex Bills, American Federation of Astrologers, Tempe AZ, 1971.

Werner Erhard by William Warren Bartley, III, Clarkson N. Potter Inc., Publishers, New York 1978.

About the Author

My own involvement with the *Inner Guide Meditation* began in 1992 when I went to see Ed Steinbrecher for what I intended to be professional information gathering and to get his take on my chart. An Astrologer myself, I heard through the grapevine Ed was a good Astrologer – I had not heard anything else.

To my amazement, Ed began asking me about my family members and was entering their names on my chart. He then began telling me how they were barometers for what was going on in my own life. I thought to myself, and then said: "This isn't what I came here for." After a few brief comments that interested me beyond a chart reading, he told me to close my eyes and to enter a cave without "watching" myself. He asked a lot of questions about the cave and then took me on an inner journey I didn't want to end. I then thought, "How cool is this!" I was hooked!

Since that time, regular meditation has proven its worth in how I choose relationships, how I conduct myself in career matters, and how I make decisions at every level. My *Inner Work* has changed my *Outer World* for the better – not without challenges, of course, but certainly with more "tools" to work through them. I trained with Ed and other D.O.M.E. instructors to be an Initiator/Counselor of the Meditation, and I encourage people to begin their own sustainable process of inner growth and outer progress with the Inner Guide Meditation early in life, if possible, or later. We have all the answers inside ourselves – we just need a tool to get them out and working for us. This one works! *Swimming in Your Brain* offers an organized system for lifetime use of the IGM, as well as other *tools* for personal and professional progress.

I am a Saturnian Vessel, formally educated in Astrological Arts & Sciences at Kepler College in Washington State and in Communications Arts & Sciences at the University of Southern California, courses at D.O.M.E. in the Inner Guide Meditation, as well as many group classes and workshops in metaphysical arts, **est**, and Integral Theory. I am also a Certified Astrological Professional of the International Society for Astrological Research (ISAR). Aside from personal development and participation in sustainable *Life Planning & Organization* for my clients and their children, my interests include the Arts in general, classical music in particular, sustainable Earth stewardship, and wild animal conservation.

May you be Star centered and Moon linked.
Elle

I invite you to join my *circle of hands* around
all living things on Earth and in the Sea to balance our energies.

Elle Simon

2012

www.Moonlinks.net

SwimmingInYourBrain@Yahoo.com

Printed in the United States
By Bookmasters